Riding The
Roller
Coaster

A Muslim Perspective on
Overcoming the Challenges of Life

Riding The Roller Coaster

A MUSLIM PERSPECTIVE ON
OVERCOMING THE CHALLENGES OF LIFE

Javed Mohammed

amana publications

First Edition
(1426AH/2005AC)

amana publications
10710 Tucker Street
Beltsville, Maryland 20705-2223 USA
Tel: (301) 595-5999 / Fax: (301) 595-5888
E-mail: amana@igprinting.com
Website: www.amana-publications.com

Library of Congress Cataloging-in-Publication Data

Mohammed, Javed, 1960-
 Riding the roller coaster : a Muslim perspective on overcoming the
challenges of life / Javed Mohammed.-- 1st ed.
   p. cm.
 Includes bibliographical references.
 ISBN 1-59008-037-8
 1. Muslims--Conduct of life. 2. Islam--Social aspects. 3. Islamic
ethics. I. Title.

 BJ1292.M87M64 2005
 297.5'7--dc22

                                            2005022762

Printed in the United States of America by International Graphics
10710 Tucker Street, Beltsville, Maryland 20705-2223
Tel: (301) 595-5999 Fax: (301) 595-5888

Website: igprinting.com
E-mail: ig@igprinting.com

CONTENTS

I begin in the name of God,
The Compassionate, The Merciful

ACKNOWLEDGMENTS

This book would not be possible without the help of God and many people; some mentioned here, others referenced, and many others who may go nameless. Specifically, those who reviewed, edited, and helped with the publication of the book deserve special mention. The editors being Souheila Aljadda, Sameena Khan, Gloria Manole, Aaisha Burney, and Amatullah Al Marwani. Also feedback from Sandy Short, Sadia Shaikh and my reference librarian friends from the Milpitas, CA library Don, Teri, Lauren and Susan. I would also like to thank Linda Widad Woodad for her mentoring and for coordinating with the sisters from the Islamic Writers Alliance who wrote poems for this book, several of which are included in the text.

Out of every hardship come lessons for human beings, so I am grateful for the ones that have come my way. Thank you to my parents, sisters, wife and children, Nasir Moinuddin, Muhammed Perwaiz, Bill and Louise and your families and all the rest of you for your support and prayers through some challenging times.

A NOTE TO THE READER

This book is about putting belief and action together to ride the emotional roller coaster of life. It is addressed to people of all faiths. The term God is used throughout the text. It is in reference to Allah, the Arabic word for The One and Only God of all humanity.

This book also includes examples from various Prophets that are recognized in the Abrahamic faiths of Judaism, Christianity and Islam. In Islam, the mention of a Prophet is followed with reverence by the words, "Peace Be Upon Him" (pbuh). For the sake of readability, this has been omitted but is implied.

A final note: In the quoted verses of the Holy Qur'an, the reader may note the word "We" refers to God. This is not to be confused with any concept of trinity or pluralism. Muslims believe God is One and the "We" is a royal plural (much in the way a king would say, "And we grant our subjects freedom in the land" even though he is talking about himself alone).

Introduction

LIFE IS ONE OPEN BOOK TEST

I don't know about you, but I have never been comfortable riding roller coasters. Yes, it can be exciting and at different ages I have gone through varying emotions. When I wasn't tall enough to ride, it was "wow, wouldn't it be nice", which later became "sure, I can handle this" and is now "let the kids go on without me"! If my attitude towards roller coasters has changed over time, then so has my attitude towards life.

When I was going to school, I felt excitement over the ending of exams and homework.

When I started my first job, I was looking forward to getting a couple more years of experience. The desire to always look forward to the next level became ingrained. I have worked for over twenty years, traveled the world, been laid-off from my job several times and started new careers. What's next?

Whereas the roller coasters in the amusement park have a clear entry and exit, the proverbial roller coaster of life continues in its endless turns and loops. The only time we get off is when life is over; otherwise, there is no getting off.

The problems you and I face may have similarities and differences. Maybe you, too, lost your job or faced a life-threatening illness. Maybe you are facing problems in your marriage, a death of a close family member, are on the verge of bankruptcy or have some other hardship. Whatever the challenge, no two individuals (even identical twins) will have exactly the same package of problems. If most of us endure and ride through these problems, we will make it the ride of our lives.

This book is about identifying the universal principles that can help us ride through the ups and downs of life. For me, it started with job loss and the Pandora's Box it opened up.

I have been fascinated by what makes people resilient. What makes, for example, someone who has gone through a health or family crisis become strong and brave enough to face the problems head on? I have turned to the Scriptures and the stories of Prophets gone by, the tales of the Sufi masters, and the examples of many contemporary people, to uncover five important principles which can help us face the challenges of life: Patience, Prayer, Purpose, Proactive Planning and Passionate Persistence. I, by no means, claim there are only five and that they all begin with the letter P; that is just to make it easier to remember. However, I am sure you will agree that these are universal principles, which, if put into action, can give us comfort and confidence to meet life head on.

Within the folds of history, there are many stories carrying examples of past generations of people who not only faced hardships but also successfully overcame them.

Over fifteen hundred years ago in a small trading town in the deserts of Arabia, a boy was born. His father died before the child drew his first breath, his mother before he reached the age of six. From there, this orphan was brought up by his grandfather who died when he was only eight. Thereafter, his uncle looked after him. Later, as an adult, he married and had six children of his own, four daughters and two sons. Both sons died in their infancy. At the age of forty, he received the Revelation of Prophethood from God. As he invited others to worship God, he was subjected to cruel and harsh punishment. This ranged from mockery to boycotts to physical assaults and finally, having a ransom on his head. His followers also faced similar persecution and torture. All his daughters except one died before him. He faced deprivation to the extent of tying stones to his stomach to kill the pangs of hunger. He slept on the floor. He had to fight for and defend his people and his belief. At the time of his death, he had little in terms of material wealth, yet he came to be viewed as the most influential man in history by not only followers, but also foes.

None of us can imagine wave after wave of tribulation like this. Who was this man? None other than the Prophet Muhammad.

Look at the life of any of the Prophets and you will see trial upon trial, from Adam to Abraham, Job to Jesus and Moses to Muhammad (may peace be upon them all). Amongst other things, they combined faith with action, patience with gratitude. They were persistent in their mission, proactively planned and went about their work with passion. These are a few of the many lessons we can learn from them.

Before we can get into discussing these principles, I should mention the prerequisite for understanding and truly benefiting from Prophets and sage men is having faith in the one God. We live in a world which is becoming more material and less spiritual, emphasizing action without faith. For example, if you lose your job, the advice many receive from outplacement centers is to get your resume in shape, practice interviewing skills, learn about negotiating salary, and other tactical issues. Is someone who has a "good" background, a great resume and outstanding interview skills assured of getting a job?

Is having an MBA or other degree from an Ivy League school an assurance you will be successful? This is not meant to be a criticism of the value of outplacement resources or having a degree from an outstanding school. These are all important experiences or skills required in getting a job. However, at the time this was written, there are scores of unemployed people even with PhDs from Ivy League universities and years of experience. Their resumes and interviewing skills speak for themselves yet they are struggling to get a minimum wage job. Many have been unemployed for over two years in the heart of the booming Silicon Valley.

My comments are not limited to the unemployed. You may be young, beautiful or handsome, come from a good family, have a good education but are struggling to get married. Maybe you are married and struggling because of your spouse, in-laws, or some other factor. Maybe you and/or your spouse are healthy and you have children with major health problems. Maybe you have led a healthy life, exercised, ate the right foods, avoided stressful activities but you were just diagnosed with high blood pressure or diabetes or worse.

All these examples are meant to illustrate one point—our rational thoughts, abilities and actions can only take us so far.

Neither I nor anyone else can explain away the problems we face individually or collectively. Granted that we are going to face hardships, how best can we plan to face them? How can we build our adversity quotient or resiliency factor? Don't worry, we are not going to get scientific here. With a similar set of problems, what makes some people drag themselves through life and others bounce through it? That's what riding the roller coaster of life is all about.

My Problems Your Promise

A Poem by AAMINAH HERNÁNDEZ

Things have not been going my way
My imperfect plans have failed again
I turn to you, knowing Your Promise
"With every difficulty there is relief"
My lack of patience has led me here
Trying to make things work out
In my time, to my desire
My hands are empty, my heart is cold
Why did I wait to come to You?
My Lord, my Only Sustainer
As Your servant I need only ask
For my every need You fulfill
The burden I bear is nothing
To the strength You will give me
My trials are small and insignificant
To what others have conquered by Your Will
Now I finally will come to You
Ablutions made, repentance on my lips
Asking only for Your Perfect Peace
To ease my suffering and troubled mind
Now I make my supplication to You
Make remembrance of Your Names
Knowing You will replace what I miss
You will return me a better value
For what You have removed from my path
Now I make the vow and promise
To trust in Your Plan, not my own
To come quickly to You with my wants
To trust in Your Design for my life

Chapter 1

PROBLEMS, PROBLEMS, PROBLEMS

This book is not just about me, it's about you and what you can do to be better prepared when you hit the rough patches of life. As you and I share this planet with over six billion people, each and every one a unique individual, there is no way I can know or solve even a minute fraction of those problems. I will list a few of the challenges I, my family, friends or those I know have faced in the hope it will trigger your own thoughts.

My parents were born in India in the late1920s. By 1947, after the Second World War had ended, India was partitioned into India, West Pakistan and East Pakistan. As my parents lived in the state of Punjab, which was itself partitioned, being Muslim meant they would have to leave their home and farming lands and migrate to Pakistan on foot and by ox-cart. It was a treacherous journey with bandits and highway robbers running amuck. Men were hacked to death and young women kidnapped, most never to be seen again.

Plagues, floods, death and disease came and took droves of victims, some while they slept, and others on the move. Although millions perished in the greatest population exchange of the last century, many, including my parents, survived. They crossed the border through the city of Lahore on the Pakistani side of the border to safety. The reason I bring up this important historical event is that my parents, like millions of other present day refugees, are eyewitnesses to the horrors of war. Even though it was for a relatively short time, the memories are etched in their minds forever. Only those who have lived through war or genocide know what it truly means. Similarly, those who have lived through the Great Depression or a major recession know what that means.

I was born in 1960 in a village about 70 miles from Lahore, Pakistan. In that time and place, immunizations were uncommon. Only months old, I contracted Polio. My mother and those who saw me had given up hope but I was destined to live. Later, I would learn that Polio has several stages of progression. The first stage can almost pass without any long term effects, the second leads to muscle waste and the third can cripple or kill. I was fortunate my disease stopped after the second stage.

After I was born, my father immigrated to Manchester, England. We (my mother, sister and I) followed later. Although I had Polio, it did not prevent me from leading a normal life; I could walk and run like all the other children. I was not aware I had skinny legs because I always wore pants (shorts being a rarity perhaps due to the cold English weather). In fact, I would run from home to the mosque, a distance of approximately three miles each way, to save my bus-fare to fund my passion of model airplane collecting.

Life proceeded normally until I started middle school at the age of eleven. Now, for the first time, I had to wear not only a school uniform, but also shorts during P.E. class. That was my first exposure to what taunts and harassment can do to your confidence and outlook. Fellow students would laugh at my skinny legs, wondering why I was like that. Jokes abounded and my nickname became "Bones". At the time, I had no explanation why I was the way I was. When it came time to pick teams for soccer or any other sports, I would usually be the last to get picked. It wasn't until high school started that most of this name-calling subsided. I learned a new sport, badminton, and although I never made it to the team, I became pretty good.

The next major transition for me happened when I was around eleven years old. My paternal grandfather died in the early 1970s and my father had to go back to Pakistan to visit. While there, the war between India and Pakistan erupted and he was delayed for a few months. Meanwhile, the terraced house we lived in was getting old and the city wanted to demolish the whole neighborhood. When my father returned, we then not only had to move, but he also had to find a job. This was the first time for him to be unemployed and also in debt. My maternal grandfather died soon after. The impact of this and our financial situation sent my mother into a depression. My mother's health had never been good; she suffered from bouts of migraines. Now the pressure was intense on my father and my older sister who took on the role of caretaker for my younger sister and me. Although we were Muslims by faith, I can't say religion played a strong role in our lives. My mother went through electric shock therapy and depression medication, with no recovery in sight. After many years of struggle, she did regain her health.

Afterwards, we changed our family physician and the new doctor observed a curvature on my foot. He felt I should have surgery; otherwise, the curvature would get worse. The orthopedic surgeon agreed and at age fourteen, I had my first surgery. Besides the stay in the hospital, returning to school with crutches was very difficult. Once again it led to taunts and being made fun of. The surgery was not successful and I developed a limp. Two years later, the procedure was repeated again, unfortunately with the same result.

I finished high school and did reasonably well, then found junior college about the same. I dreamed of going to the United States. I started getting information and applying for colleges. Much to my dismay, I found I would not be able to afford it. I managed to gain admission in my hometown's Manchester University to study Computer Engineering. I found my self with a different class of people. I had not anticipated the level of students and competition. Many of the English students came from elite grammar or private schools. There were overseas students who were also the best and brightest. Needless to say, I struggled through my freshman year. I failed some of the exams and had to re-take them in summer. It was all or nothing; if I did not pass I would be thrown out of college. I managed not only to survive this but thrived in the coming two years to graduate.

During this time, although totally unplanned, I was introduced to a young lady barely out of high school. I always thought I would wait until I was working, but it somehow happened. The next thing I knew, I was a married college student. Study was at the forefront as the early years of marriage went by quickly. I also discovered Muslim students from other parts of the world. After listening to religious sermons and seeing the practicality of this faith, I started becoming closer to Islam.

After finishing university, I finally got the opportunity to visit the United States. I was so excited, I skipped the graduation. This was a low budget, high risk travel across America by bus. A friend and I decided to meet up in New York, visit, and travel to various destinations as we made our way to Los Angeles. That is a story for another book since it was such an interesting adventure.

After I returned to England, I dreamt many times of the scenic countryside in Connecticut and would long to go back there. I started to work full time, first near London and then in Manchester. After about three years of work, I faced my first layoff. I was given a three-month notice to look for another job. I had always wanted to move to the United States and had been applying in the many months that had preceded, but to no avail. At this very time when I needed it the most, I received a call to go for an interview to Sunnyvale, California. The twist was that even though it was a US company, the initial job assignment would be in Tokyo. Although the idea of visiting Japan seemed intriguing, I did not see much benefit in going there as my heart was in America. At the same time, I had already been offered a job in Boston to work for a defense contractor. Going to work on the East Coast was not very appealing but it seemed like my ticket to the US. I called in prayer for God's guidance to show me the better way. It turned out to be Japan and I never looked back and never thought about questioning the One who Knows what is best.

What turned out to be a layoff ended up being my dream job in computer design. I had always wondered when the British engineers came back from Japan, what it would be like riding the Shinkansen bullet train. Now, not only did I get to ride it once in a while, I lived about 100 yards from the Shinkansen line. At night, I would take my infant son and show him the sparks generated from the electrified lines that powered the bullet trains. It was like a mini fourth of July whenever we wanted.

I worked for seven years for Amdahl with three assignments in Japan. During the third and final assignment, when I got back from Japan to Sunnyvale, I was laid off. Rumors had been traveling that something was pending, but it happened suddenly. I was asked to pack my belonging and be out of the office by noon. After leaving the building I headed straight to my refuge, the mosque. It gave me time to contemplate before I headed home. When I told my wife, she was very understanding. I regrouped and decided to use the benefits the company provided. I was fortunate to go through outplacement and it helped me to prepare for the job market. By interacting with other people who had been laid off, not only did I find some camaraderie, but I also found out about the lives other people were living. Although seven years (by Silicon Valley standards) seemed like a long time, there were people who had worked their entire careers there. This was their only life…this was their family…and this is where they had put their faith. Besides feeling betrayed, they were at a loss for whom to turn to.

What I learned at the outplacement center was invaluable. I started a job-search workshop and weekly meetings in the mosque to help others who weren't educated in this aspect. It was almost ironic; here I was, out of a job, while educating others on how to get a job.

What benefit came out of this layoff? I had learned about marketing and was fascinated by this type of job. Besides, marketing folks had nice offices and free coffee. But whenever I approached marketing management, I was told I did not have the right kind of background. Determined, I started to spread the word I was interested in leaving engineering for a move to marketing. I received skeptical responses. However, one person forwarded my resume to the marketing manager in his department at AMD in Sunnyvale, California. I had started taking classes in marketing and this, along with the good reference and the booklets I'd written on my personal experiences, helped me land the job. It was not an easy transition from mainframes to PCs, from systems to chips, from engineering to marketing, but I managed to ride the roller coaster. After three years, I got a job as a marketing manager at Toshiba America and helped to start and drive the networking business. There were many changes in both the top management as well as my immediate management. In six years, I must have easily gone through about a dozen bosses. Although change always brought fear and uncertainty, I thrived there with some bosses who recognized my talents. I traveled many times to Japan and Europe as well as within the US. I had the dream six-figure salary (just for clarification it was in the lower six figures!).

As the years went by, the economy went into a recession. My company and division followed the downward spiral. Once again, I ended up on the firing line and was let go with many other employees. Once again, I knew the routine: pack up my belongings and make a quiet exit. I said goodbye to some colleagues and wished them well. I did not know they, too, were to be receiving similar news.

I do not think we can totally be prepared for what life hits us with, but some things do have foreshadowing. My boss who had helped me blossom, had left a few months before I was laid off and left me 'orphaned' for a time. The revenue picture was clearly bad yet I thought, like so many times in the past, we would ride through it. I had received calls from recruiters and had turned them down. Now, I thought how *foolish of me!* Didn't I see the writing on the wall? Again, my refuge after leaving the building was to head straight to the mosque.

As on the previous occasion, I did not waste time and joined the outplacement services offered by the company. It gave me a place to go; my routine of dropping off the children at school and then going to my "new office" did not change. Only this office was the outplacement center. I took all the classes there I could; met with my consultant once in a while, followed the daily practice of looking for and applying for jobs and searching for networking opportunities. I was also enrolled in a job search work team where fellow unemployed professionals got together. Each week, we would have to provide a status update and when relevant, ask for advice from others.

When my six months expired with the outplacement, I began to attending government job centers. This not only got me away from home, it also allowed me to have a routine.

Although I had a few interviews, there were no follow-up interviews and surely no offers. I wanted to stay away from marketing of semiconductor chips. I wanted to do something more meaningful, maybe non-profit. Regardless of what type of job I applied for or how relevant my experience was, it never seemed to be enough. My expectations were lowered from my previous six-figure salary job to minimum wage.

There you have it, down and out at forty plus. Either too much experience or too little for whatever the employer was looking for in an employee.

Later I learned about a startup which had almost finished developing a software product and needed help with marketing. I took the job on an equity only basis. This meant no salary but it was an opportunity to stay busy, make a mark and learn something I would not have had the opportunity to do otherwise.

With each layoff, though the time to get a job has been longer, I feel I have come out much stronger as a person.

When we are faced with a hardship, it is very difficult to see what the benefit is in it. Once it passes by, it's easier to reflect. Think about the hardships you have faced. How have you come through them? What are the side benefits you received from them?

For me, my first layoff landed me in business class on a trip first to the US and then Japan, a down payment on a house and a great cultural experience. My second layoff got me a job in marketing and made me a more well-rounded person. My third layoff, ok...that's a tougher one! Seriously though, it's given me pause to reflect on what my life is about. It has allowed me to acquire new skills at an executive position in a software startup. It has allowed my family and I to start living more frugally, to give away more of what we have (and don't use), to buy what we really need and to give appreciation for the things we used to take for granted like health insurance.

If riding the roller coaster is about hitting the tough spots of life and riding through them, then what can we expect? Although some problems in life (health or financial issues, for example) are very common, others are not. Many of the traumas I have spoken about like being a victim of crime, kidnap, murder or terrorism are not just headline news—these are people you may know directly or indirectly. You have probably heard of the six degrees of separation, that most if not all people can be reached through six levels of contacts. For many situations, I think it can be even less.

My family and friends are split across three continents. I have lived in middle class neighborhoods and do not come from a dysfunctional family. Yet, I know of someone close who was either kidnapped, murdered, attacked and so forth. I know of people who were madly in love and ended up in bizarre and non-amicable divorces. I know of families with good values yet their children are drug-pushers. Some committed suicide and other lives ended suddenly.

How do you tell a young mother with six children why her working class husband was robbed and shot at point-blank range in his own home in front of his children? What do you say to the parents of a two year old who has been diagnosed with cancer? What do you say to a neighbor's family whose daughter has been assaulted? I am sure you have heard the news and numbers but these are a sampling of real people facing real hardship that I know personally. I am sure if you think about it you will find yourself or others in these and other adversities.

Life is full of adversities but it is also full of hope and goodness. This, in the end, is what makes the world carry on. The following chapters share universal principles, inspirational stories and practical ideas to make the principles into reality. Prayer. Patience. Purpose. Proactive planning. Passionate persistence. Your ticket to riding the roller coaster of life.

I'm only human

A Poem by VEILED WRITER

Walking through doors
In between hoping and coping
Through difficulty,
Positivity and Creativity

> Hanging on the wall
> In front of me Faith
> I build upon it
> Through falling Down
> And getting back Up

Believing, It's not easy
But it strengthens me
Like the roots of a Palm tree
Running deep Into the ground
Bringing forth shade
For those in need of it

> I know Mistakes will be made
> Abundantly Even
> I believe in
> Have faith in
> The Merciful One
> Who created me

Every thing happens for a reason and
With each season
I fall down And get back up
To continue to walk through doors
Faithfully
For I'm only human and this is
The way for me

Chapter 2

ALL YOU NEED IS PRAYER

As a Muslim, I am required to pray five times a day: dawn, noon, late afternoon, after sunset and finally, at night. Each prayer takes about five to fifteen minutes. Although the hardest has to be getting up at dawn, each has its own joy. Due to work and other distance limitations, I am usually only able to go to the mosque for the morning and evening prayers as well as the Friday congregational prayer. The required ablution (washing hands, face, arms, and feet) gives me a great cooling and relaxing start to each prayer. It also gives an automatic break to work and, yes, boring meetings.

What do these obligatory prayers do for me? They are a form of meditation, a chance to disconnect even for a short period with the worldly woes and connect with the One who has power over all woes. They give me a sense of fulfillment that I am hopefully pleasing my Creator. At times, when my mind isn't adrift (and truthfully, it does wander), I am able to focus on the words of the prayer. In the first chapter of the Qur'an, called *Surah Al-Fatiha* or The Opening (which is very similar to the Lord's Prayer), the verses are heart-lifting and call out for a response..."(O, God!) You alone we worship and You alone we seek from for help." Pondering this keeps me from being drowned by my problems, keeps me thinking about the One who can help alleviate them.

THE POWER OF PRAYER

In this life, we are exposed to calamities, problems and crises. Some we overcome and others overcome us. We may feel knocked down, helpless, brokenhearted or hit by other disabling emotions. Maybe you have recently divorced, lost a loved one, did not marry the person you wanted. Maybe you did not get a promotion, lost your job or money. Whatever the situation, there is one important factor all people defer back to at moments of crisis and that is to religion and God, through prayer.

Prayers are of different kinds in different faiths. Some are prayers of worship, others of supplication and still others of giving thanks. It is the innate nature of the human being to turn to God at times of distress. All humans have a subconscious awareness God exists. Even the staunch atheist will say "Oh God" when the plane suddenly starts to drop or hit turbulence. However, prayer is not something saved for times of distress only. In Islam, a Muslim is required to pray five times a day. Besides this, there are many other prayers of supplication, thanks and asking for help.

Whatever your religious beliefs, we call unto a Supreme Being— the creation calls on their Creator. When problems appear bigger than life, we all turn to that one entity, God. A sincere prayer for guidance or help is all it takes. It entails asking for the best in our affairs for this world and the hereafter, for the short term and the long term. From an Islamic perspective, all prayers are accepted. These may come in the form of visible results or in results which are deferred, in terms of alleviating a forthcoming hardship or being rewarded in the hereafter.

Our prayers have one thing in common, the belief of a power far greater than us. A power that is so great we cannot comprehend it. Yet it comprehends all and created the universe and all it contains. This supreme being has the answers to all questions: why we exist, what lies beyond death, why there is so much apparent injustice in this world, why there will be true justice in the next. A divine attribute of God is that He is *Al-Mu'min*, the Inspirer of Faith. He is the Comforter and Protector of the one who takes refuge in Him.

"Pray to me and I will hear your prayer," says the Qur'an (40:60).

Each of us may have our favorite prayers. There are two from many verses in the Qur'an which help me put things in perspective and show me a way to ask for assistance. There are many other prayers but at times of tribulation this prayer is the first anchor or foundation I, and anyone who chooses, can turn to: "O you who believe! Seek assistance through patience and prayer; surely God is with the patient. And We will most certainly try you with somewhat of fear and hunger and loss of property and lives and fruits; and give good news to the patient, who, when a misfortune befalls them, say: Surely we are God's and to Him we shall surely return. Those are they on whom are blessings and mercy from their Lord, and those are the followers of the right course." (Qur'an 2.153, 155-157)

These verses call out to the believers in God and let us know we can expect different kinds of hardships. Here is another powerful example of seeking help: "God does not impose upon any soul a burden but to the extent of its ability; for it is (the benefit of) what it has earned and upon it (the evil of) what it has wrought. (Pray:) Our Lord! Do not punish us if we forget or make a mistake; Our Lord! Do not lay on us a burden as Thou didst lay on those before us; Our Lord! Do not impose upon us that which we have not the strength to bear and pardon us and grant us protection and have mercy on us. Thou art our Patron, so help us against those who hide the truth." (Qur'an 2.286)

As with any prayer, it must be based on sound belief and pure intentions. It can be aided by giving in charity and this applies both in good and bad times. Although giving in good times may seem obvious, it is giving in bad times that has intrigued me. Giving, whether it is of money or service, has a way of not only finding its way back, but the joy and satisfaction it gives cannot be put into words.

Prayer is not a stand-alone activity. Faith and action must go hand in hand. To get a job, having a good resume and interview skills are important…and so is prayer. If one is sick, taking medication is important but taken with prayer, one experiences complete healing. This is something that should be taught in medical schools as there is plenty of research to back this up.

There are many examples of Prophets and righteous people using the power of prayer. For example, when Prophet Abraham was thrown into the fire because he had destroyed the idols as his faith instructed him, he prayed to God who answered by commanding the fire to be cool. Prayer is a powerful tool. How little we use it! It can be done individually and collectively. All blessings come from God, so we must surely ask Him for help.

Prayer helps in healing of all types. It allows you to take a spiritual vacation from worldly problems. Muslims are commanded in their faith to pray five times a day. A ritual washing of the hands, face, arms and feet precedes each prayer. It allows the individual to reconnect with God and receive a spiritual charge. It also cools the pressure points in the body which stimulates calmness. It provides a physical and mental break from daily stress. The physical movements of salah (Muslim prayer) stretch and energize the body. The spiritual aspect moves one to stop worrying and turn to a greater power on Whom we all depend. It allows us not to worry about things we have no control over.

PERSONAL PRAYERS AT WORK

Although I have always believed in God and have been raised as a Muslim, my closeness to faith took a turn when I went to college. There, for the first time, I came into contact with other Muslim students, many from different parts of the world. Although I was familiar with the rituals of prayer, hearing the heart-touching recitation of the Qur'an from a Turkish student made me want to not only keep listening but also to start learning how to read it in a similar manner. For the first time, I started to understand from the Friday sermons the real application and understanding of Islam. Hearing about what will happen on the Day of Judgment and the Hereafter in graphic detail from inspiring speakers brought me closer to my faith.

After Ramadan, the month of fasting, I went to visit a friend and noticed through the window that he was praying. Although I had known I should pray five times a day everyday I did not. I, too, started to pray regularly out of sheer envy.

Later on, while at work or outside the home, I would pray sitting, not having the knowledge or confidence to pray in the various standing and sitting positions. When I reflect back on that time, some prayers stand out. Once, while facing tough family issues, I called unto God and sincerely asked for His help. I felt we were falling apart. However, through His mercy, we pulled together.

Another was a major decision point in my life. I wanted to live and work in the United States for the longest time. After many years of perseverance, it finally came through. I had a job offer but it wasn't my dream location or position. While my immigration was being started, I received a call from another recruiter who wanted me to interview for an American company. This was to be in Sunnyvale, California, for a position which had an assignment in Japan. Although going to California and working for a computer designer was very interesting, I had no desire to go to Japan. My wife was pregnant and I thought to myself, why waste two years in Japan? I made the optional prayer for guidance. The inclination after this prayer came in favor of Japan and that's where I packed my bags for and left. Once my wife delivered, I picked her and my six-week-old son up for a sixteen hour flight from London to Tokyo via Anchorage and I have never looked back. It was a beneficial decision, both as an experience in a different culture and financially, too.

The next prayer which stands out in my mind is the prayer my father, my wife and I made at the Mountain of Mercy, near Mecca during *Hajj* (the pilgrimage) in 1991. *Hajj* is a once in a life time journey which all adult Muslims should do if they can afford to and are in good health. My father had been to Mecca once before and was familiar with what to do. The Mountain of Mercy is the place where Muslims believe Prophet Adam and Eve were reunited on earth, where Adam made prayers to God. My father made some of the most heart warming supplications I ever heard. When I was younger, my father told me many of the blessings we were receiving were from Allah answering my grandfather's prayers. I truly believe those and others carried me through, in spite of all my shortcomings.

If there's one other prayer I would like to share, it is the following. As I was writing the manuscript for this book, my three-year-old daughter, Nadia, in her adventures around the house, managed to find a mechanical pencil belonging to my fourteen-year-old daughter, Aliyah. Nadia pulled it apart and the lead from the pencil fell on the carpet. Later, when Aliyah returned from school, her foot landed on one of those pieces which became embedded in her heel. The doctor said to give it time but that made little difference to the pain. Eventually, the doctor tried to pry it out, but to no avail. She then referred us to a surgeon who could take it out under a local anesthetic. We set up the appointment and I expected this to be a walk-in, procedure. Little did I know it would require full anesthesia and surgery in the hospital. All for a small piece of pencil-lead, which was causing pain and aggravation. During this time, my father-in-law died so my wife and Nadia went to visit her family in Pakistan. Later, I was told by the doctor's secretary the insurance had approved the surgery. We were all set for the big day. When I went to register at the hospital, the administrator said she did not have the approval. She said she would make a note of it and to proceed with the surgery since everything else was set to go.

My daughter went and was prepped for the surgery and the anesthesia started. At that point I had to leave her and went back to the administrator. When she called the insurance, her jaw dropped and I could tell there was bad news pending. The insurance had not approved the surgery and had instead requested the surgery be cancelled! Being unemployed and not knowing how expensive the bill would be, I worked up a sweat. Fearing the worst, I asked if my daughter could be pulled out of the surgery but I was told it was too late.

When the administrator moved away, I prayed to God for His help. In the longest twenty minutes I know, I saw a different response from the administrator. This time there was an approval number at the end of it. As I went to the waiting room, I was overcome with so much happiness and gratitude that I once again performed my ablution and stood in prayer. For the first time in two years after having been laid off, I broke down in my prayer. I am not one who cries easily. Even at moments of joy, I have held myself. Islam makes it easier for me to exercise humility. Two years prior, I was earning a nice six figure salary. I never had to worry about money and spent in good ways as generously as I could. Now, here I was reduced to rubble.

One should never say life is bad or could not get worse. Just a couple of weeks later, the same daughter, Aliyah, had an appointment with an orthopedic specialist. My wife discovered Aliyah's back was showing some irregularity. For many years, the pediatrician said it would go away. I prayed this visit would not bring bad news. Looking at the X-rays and Aliyah, the doctor said this disorder is called Scoliosis, a curvature of the backbone. Although a brace could be an option, the most likely cure would have to be major surgery of the back. My heart sank and my feet could hardly carry my weight.

Having undergone surgery on my foot twice and not coming out of it well, I continued to hope it would not come to that for our daughter. A follow up visit to a specialist confirmed the first dreaded opinion. As much as I was praying Aliyah would not need surgery, it appeared to be the most likely option. My family and I were solaced by the fact there was hope. We have access to some of the best medical facilities. Our children have state covered insurance which would cover a great portion of the costs. It is one thing to be in pain, but seeing the pain of your own children is even harder.

When Aliyah was younger, she would break into tears when I had to leave for a business trip. At the moment of separation as she was about to go into a six hour surgery, it was I who fell apart. "God be with you, baby girl, be strong" my own voice quavered. It was the longest wait I can remember and the thought of what the surgeon may be doing was unbearable. Seeing the surgeon, Dr. Rinsky, come to greet us post-surgery with a smile on his face was comforting. Seeing Aliyah afterwards even more so, even though she broke out in a Harry Potter accent, which confused the anesthetists. Slowly, she was allowed to move from chewing ice to drinking clear liquids and finally to solid food. In the days to come, back spasms and pain were some-what expected but a new complication arose. She couldn't hold food down and had no bowel movements, a concern for the medical team. Again all food and liquid was cut. I was reminded of the value and benefit of things we take for granted. As a family, we started to pray.

It reminded me of the story of Haroon Rashid (a famous *Caliph* or Muslim ruler) who was asked by an advisor, "If you were dying of thirst and somebody was willing to offer you a glass of water, what would it be worth?" Haroon answered, "Half of my kingdom." Then, his advisor asked, "And if you drank the water and could not dis-charge it (ie could not urinate), and somebody offered you a cure, what would that be worth?" Haroon answered, "The other half of my kingdom." The advisor commented, "Then what is the worth of this kingdom?!" I could see how my daughter and I would be willing first to give anything so she could drink or eat and second, to be able to discharge it.

Now I reflect back and see not having a job was a minor incon-venience. Is every prayer answered? As a Muslim I believe God answers them, although it is not always apparent in what way, shape or form.

There you have it. Prayer is powerful, it can move mountains, it can help us conquer our galactic fears and fulfill our deepest desires. All you need is a sincere prayer.

My Prayers

A Poem by RENEE WARNER

I prostrate towards Mecca for the third time today
Taking the loneliness away
Purifying me once again
Keeping me from sin.

I ache to be closer to Him
Closer than I've ever been
I long to feel complete
Then tears and Earth meet.

I thank You for Your gift.
Through these thoughts I sift.
And regain focus on You.
I know my faith is true.

Accept my Prayers O Lord.
Forgive me O Lord
Guide me O Lord.
Help me O Lord

I ask You why You chose to guide me?
I can't see.
Although I accept Your trust
For You must see something I don't. You must.

Now I ask in my Supplication
Help the state of this nation.
Let them see You as we Muslims do
The reason for living is only You.

Help those who can't see
that believing in You
is their only hope
to cope.

It's a sad state of affairs here on Earth today.
You see it so I don't have to say.
Help us through this life
And strife.

In this Prayer
I ask You "Please keep me with You."
In reality, It's all I ask of You.

Chapter 3

THE DRIVE FOR PATIENCE

Did you know there are 99 divine attributes of God and that one of them is patience? According to a Prophetic saying, patience is half of faith. Patience is one of the most frequently mentioned qualities God asks the believers to practice along with prayer in times of hardship.

The Qur'an says, "…and be patient (have *Sabr*) and persevering: for God is with those who patiently preserve." (8: 46)

Sabr is an Arabic word which has a much richer meaning than the word patience. Linguistically, *Sabr* means detain, refrain and stop. In the Islamic terminology, *Sabr* means to stop oneself from despairing and panicking. To stop one's tongue—from complaining—and hands—from striking—at times of grief or stress. Just as patience means holding back, it also implies moving forward with courage and perseverance. Some situations do not require action like being stuck in traffic where there is little else to do but pause and wait it out. Others may require action. If someone is hurt physically or emotionally, they need attention. For others situations, for example if someone close to us gets angry, wisdom may be required to see what is the best course of action. One point that should be emphasized is patience does not mean being fatalistic. We must always do our part and complete what is our responsibility.

When things come upon us, like illness or inconvenience, we must exercise patience. There are other places where we have a choice like refraining from that which is prohibited by law. When this deals with faith, patience has a higher virtue.

Patience is a key to success and triumph. It is the ability to accept pain, trouble, misfortune or other annoyance without complaint or losing faith. It is necessary at the point when misfortune strikes. We can achieve this by a change of attitude, place or preoccupation, by prayer, or by changing the immediate conditions around us

Patience means having trust in God. Especially in those matters where we have no choice, a calamity or disaster like an accident or death or other types of loss. When we are afflicted, we know this is a test and relief will only come from Him. Everyone's test is a little different so one of the things to avoid is comparisons. People may seem to be happy from the outside but only the individual, God and anyone they share their grief with really knows their true situation.

God tests us in different ways to show who is true in his faith and who is false. He sees who puts Him above himself and all other beings in this world. He knows who dedicates himself to the pleasures of this life and forgets about God and the Last Day. The Qur'an says, "Do people think that they will be left alone on saying, 'We believe', and that they will not be tested. We did test those before them and God will certainly know those who are true from those who are false." (29:2-3).

The Prophet Muhammad said, "The case of the believer is wonderful; there is good for him in everything, and this characteristic is exclusively for him alone. If he experiences something pleasant, he is grateful to God and that is good for him; and if he comes across some adversity, he is patient and submissive and that is also good for him."

It is unfortunate that we live in a world, which due to its

technologies and advancements, is becoming more impatient. We have many conveniences in life providing us with instant satisfaction. Yet, the reality of the world is gradual gratification. For example, a farmer cannot expect to harvest the crop if he does not sow the seed, water it, nurture it and wait for it to grow into a healthy plant.

Patience is a muscle that has to be exercised often. The more it is worked, the stronger we become to face the hardships of life. By connecting with God and depending on Him, we will not despair in life. Especially when one looses a loved one, the believer is encouraged to say, "All of us belong to God and all of us will return to Him." It is natural to cry and feel sad but we should not object to God's decree. From a Muslim perspective, having difficulties, including sickness, can have benefit. It can purify us from our wrong actions.

Withholding anger and having forgiveness when dealing with people are key qualities that can assist in being patient. Another important quality that relates to patience is gratitude. Gratitude means giving thanks to the giver of the favor whether it is God or another person. Gratitude stands for thanking the conferrer for his graces and using them in the ways that would please the giver.

Gratitude can be expressed by the heart, verbally or by action, one leading to the next. Whatever favor we have been blessed with— money, knowledge, position—we have to use all or part of it as an expression of gratitude. Think of the blessings God has bestowed each of us with and look at those who are in more difficult situations than we are in, as well as the calamities and illnesses from which God has saved us. Every single twinkling of the eye, every single word that is spoken, every single movement of an organ and every single breath— all these are great favors of God that none can appreciate except those who are deprived of them.

Patience is a quality we must develop and exercise often in the roller coaster of life.

ME PATIENT? TRYING AND CAN DO BETTER!

This book is not meant to be theoretical; I do not plan to preach to you what I do not practice myself. As much as we ask others to be patient, it is in reality not an easy thing to practice. I can honestly say, though, I do not know of a situation when I let the handle fly loose (that is I got angry) where afterwards I did not regret and apologize for it.

Do I have some stories about myself or a close family member about being patient? Just thinking of examples requires patience! There are some situations where we involuntarily become patient. Sitting in traffic comes to mind. I live in the San Francisco Bay Area, and like many of the other larger metropolitan areas (think Los Angeles, New York or your own town during rush-hour), traffic is a part of life.

However, nothing prepared me for the kind of traffic I experienced when I went for the Pilgrimage to Mecca on the *Hajj*. With two to three million Muslims from all over the world descending on Mecca, the logistics have been compared to coordinating twenty Super Bowls (or World Cups) at one time. Although during the *Hajj* most of the events are phased so not all the millions have to be at one place at one time, the gathering in the valley of Arafat is one event where everyone is gathered and then has to leave by the sunset prayer. Imagine three million people leaving by bus and foot at one time. The Pilgrimage commemorates the time and life of Prophet Abraham. Running between the hills of Safa and Marwa commemorates his wife, Hagar, running to look for water for her child. Being prepared to sacrifice his son, Ishmael, is commemorated in the sacrifice of an animal and the distribution of the meat to the poor.

In the valley of Mina, Muslims from different parts of the world gathered and camped together. Although we were Americans and each country had its own camp, there was still a lot of social interaction with other Muslims. This is where Malcolm X's famous letter from Mecca was written. The following is a short excerpt.

"Never have I witnessed such sincere hospitality and overwhelming spirit of true brotherhood as is practiced by people of all colors and races here in this ancient Holy Land, the home of Abraham, Muhammad and all the other Prophets of the Holy Scriptures. For the past week, I have been utterly speechless and spellbound by the graciousness I see displayed all around me by people of all colors."

Some of the tents had fans but they seemed to do little more than re-circulate the desert heat. If that was not enough, other fans right in front of our eyes swayed from side to side until they finally stopped working, their motors worn and overheated. Why complain? And for that matter, who to complain to? Although some people complained I was most impressed by the convert American Muslims. It would be easy for them to complain, but I did not see the slightest gesture. Later, when we boarded the buses at mid-night for the journey to Medina, we waited from mid-night to the early morning. The driver and some of the officials would go back and forth with our passports, counting heads and carrying on discussions in Arabic which I could not comprehend. Finally, in the early hours of the morning, the bus moved and all of us Muslims from the US, UK, Australia and other places were overjoyed. The joy was short lived. Thirty minutes later, the bus stopped for several hours. Maybe the bus driver was tired? Either way, we waited. This journey of approximately 300 kilometers which should take about three to four hours started and stopped too many times to count. We reached Medina twenty-five hours later. I was happy just to be able to get my passport back. Sitting in traffic, although no fun, to me seems trivial and I cannot understand why some people become so anxious. By staying calm and accepting a situation you have little or no control over, you avoid getting stressed and keep those around you also in good cheer. If that's you behind me, please don't honk; I was just reminiscing on the virtues of being patient!

Another example that comes to mind about patience is marriage and family. There are so many aspects about marriage (before it and during it) to dwell on. Start with finding the "right" marriage partner. I know of many people who are being passed over for marriage despite being endowed with education, good family, beauty, a profession or whatever facets potential suitors desire. Perhaps one example of a neighbor's daughter exemplifies this. She was a beautiful woman with a good family background, educated. In fact, the words of my sister describing her still resonate with me, "the ideal specimen." Yet she had difficulty getting married. Most parents hope their children will obtain a good education, get married and settle down. As the years wear on, the harder it becomes. My family and I have been there, too.

On a family related note, no doubt some issues (especially when they involve the extended family) can become complicated and are real. Meanwhile, others start off as trivial issues which snowball into something unreal. When we have guests over for dinner, I have always, due to my upbringing, liked to have good food but to keep it simple. My wife is of a different school. She will spend at least two, if not more, days preparing. The fact that she is a good cook really helps but it has been a source of irritation and contention. Each time guests were to come, we would argue over the menu. Now, I know some of you sane minded readers must be saying, "What's your problem, she's cooking, you get to eat, can't be a bad deal?!" but life is not always that rational.

Let me give you another example. I enjoy writing. I have never made money on it, certainly not on the last two books. My wife wants me to keep writing as a hobby for retirement and focus on getting paid work. This book, therefore, started off as a "classified" project. Unfortunately, word leaked out when I sent it for review. It came in through the all-reliable 'spouse-channel' that I was working on a book. Although I took the fifth amendment and pleaded that I could not confirm or deny I was doing such a thing, the peace did not last for long. As the rumors were confirmed, to say it caused a serious argument would be an understatement. How do you prevent a nuclear meltdown in marriage? My new theory: the half-life of all problems in a sane marriage decreases with the length of the marriage. After more than two decades of marriage, we have learned that some things are not worth fighting over. I let her pick the menu (after all, she does the cooking) and me...well, I am writing one more book. Other trivial problems find easier solutions like seeing the disgust on my wife's face when I would let water accumulate in the soap dish. Resolution? Thank God for liquid soap! Eureka! Life is bliss.

Last but not least, if my wife or I just hold ourselves at the point of a conflict and save the discussion for our evening walks, it seems that many problems can be resolved then or thereafter. There you have it. Be patient, use liquid soap, take walks in the evening and stick around. Your life, too, can be as satisfying as ours. There are no easy answers to the challenges of life. Everyone has their own test. Prayers and patience carry you through.

The Drive for Patience

A Poem by AMATULLAH AL-MARWANI

On my drive for patience, I take a wrong turn.
Roar through the intersection of Angry Street and Shame Avenue.
Dead end?
Reverse.

> On my drive for patience, I get lost.
> Wander around the neighborhood of guilt.
> Cul-de-sac?
> Turn left.

On my drive for patience, I break down.
Panicky search for The Mechanic.
Always open?
A call away.

> On my drive for patience, I pick up passengers.
> Buckle repentance into the front seat, trust and love in the back.
> Need a ride?
> Hop in.

On my drive for patience, I forget my map.
Ask Someone for directions.
Straight Path?
This way.

> On my drive for patience, I finally arrive.
> Engine running, I'll go down this road again.
> Short-cut?
> Let Him steer!

PARAGONS OF PATIENCE

If history is the fuel of the future, it is because it can teach us many lessons. What does history teach us about patience? There is perhaps no better example in ancient times than the Prophet Job who is recognized both in the Bible and the Qur'an as an example of one who practiced patience in adversity. His story is fascinating...

Satan became envious of Job due to the praise he received from the angels. Satan then set about to destroy Job. When all Job's possessions were ruined, he was asked by Satan (who appeared as a wise old man) if this was due to Job's habit of giving away much in charity. Satan prompted that God could have prevented this disaster of a loss of wealth if He had wanted to.

Job's reply was, "What God has taken away from me belongs to Him. I was only its trustee for a while. He gives to whom He wills and withholds from whom He wills." With these words, Job prostrated to his Lord.

Next Satan shook the foundation of the house in which Job's children were living and sent the building crashing, killing all of them. Satan acted the sympathizer and told Job his prayers were not being rewarded.

Again, Job disappointed him by replying, "God sometimes gives and sometimes takes. He is sometimes pleased and sometimes displeased with our deeds. Whether a thing is beneficial or harmful to me, I will remain firm in my belief and remain thankful to my Creator." Then Job prostrated to his Lord. At this Satan became even angrier.

Finally, Satan went after Job's health, until Job was reduced to skin and bones. But Job patiently bore the hardship and remained hopeful. Everyone except his wife deserted him. Satan made his final pass and went to the wife and reminded her of the good days. The painful memories were too much for her and she asked Job to ask God to remove their suffering. Even at this, Job reminded her the good times had lasted 80 years and this time of seven years was insignificant. The marital argument grew and his wife also left him. In this helpless state, Job turned to God, not to complain, but to seek His mercy, "Verily, distress has seized me and You are the Most Merciful of all those who show mercy." The Qur'an says, "So We answered his call, and We removed the distress that was on him, and We restored his family to him (that he had lost), and the like thereof along with them - as a mercy from Ourselves and a Reminder for all who worship Us." (21: 83-84)

Though the story of a Prophet and the duel that takes place with Satan, there are many lessons to be drawn from it for our own lives. Losses of wealth, children or health are all tribulations we can and do face. Having a firm resolve and being patient are the keys to ultimate success.

In contemporary times, there are other examples. Mahatma Gandhi used non-violence first to address the civil rights problems in South Africa and then used a similar approach to free India from British colonialism. When violent conflicts did start, he went on hunger strike to stand for his beliefs and principles.

Similarly Nelson Mandela was so strongly opposed to Apartheid in South Africa that he spent 27 years in prison for his beliefs and did not compromise them. It was his desire for the freedom of his people to live their lives with dignity and self-respect; he was willing to do whatever it took to accomplish that goal. In 1990, he took the long walk to freedom not only as a free man but also as the leader of his people.

Job, Gandhi and Mandela are examples of those who patiently persevered.

The Corner of Hope & Mercy

A Poem by AMATULLAH AL-MARWANI

Hope and Mercy are two streets in my town.
I stand at their intersection, staring down.

> I don't deserve either, neither due to me.
> I'm hardly the kind to earn God's bounty.

I sin and then, turning, boldly sin again.
If there's trouble to find, I jump right in.

> Hope and Mercy are two streets, crossed.
> How can I be here and still be lost?

I scan the crowd; do others feel this, too?
Are they also seeking a way out or through?

> In the distance, a spire rises, a voice rings out.
> "Come to your good." What is this about?

Hope and Mercy are two streets in the middle.
Does their presence solve my purpose's riddle?

> I can't wait here forever, not even all day.
> Choose soon, be on my way.

I follow the call, footsteps gathering speed.
"Come to your good"…something I need.

> Hope and Mercy are two streets I roam.
> Though on their corner, the place is home.

Body in motion, seeking God's favor.
Determined to stand, I will not waver.

> Come to your prayer, come to your good.
> Accept the invitation, if only you would.

Hope and Mercy are two streets I know.
Gifts from Above for all down below.

Chapter 4

LIVING LIFE ON PURPOSE

"**W**hat is the purpose of life?" This has to be one of the most popular questions mankind has asked and will continue to ask. As human beings, no matter how great our scientific and technical achievements, our reference will always be how we fit into God's creation. Once we understand our purpose in life, we can reframe our situation with reference to that.

If our true purpose is something different than our perceived purpose in life, immersion in work or play becomes secondary. If we know life is a test, we can avoid the trap of "Why me?" when adversity strikes. There is reward for those who believe, are patient, pray and do good which is balanced with justice for those who don't. On the journey of life, as long as our destination is clear, hitting some obstruction and taking detours is okay because we can get back on the track.

So what is the purpose of life? Depending on whom you ask, you will get a different answer. My purpose as a Muslim is to obey God, enjoin the good (while doing it!) and forbid the wrong.

Having a clear purpose in life gives it both mission and meaning. Besides the higher purpose, we must be able to translate what this means to us. We all want to be more than a "cog" that works but has no idea what it is working for. Ask yourself: *What are the unique gifts I have been endowed with? What lasting need can I fulfill? What do I live for? What am I willing to die for? What do I want to be remembered for?* These are all questions that help us answer our purpose in life. I want to take my experiences and use my writing and marketing skills to make a difference in people's lives. This, I hope, acts as a perpetual reward in the hereafter. Pause and think about the purpose of your life. Purpose, besides giving direction and other benefits, also allows us to change our situation.

PURPOSE - MY MOTIVATOR IN LIFE

Being conscious of my faith and reflecting on my life, has made it much easier for me to define my purpose. I have already spoken about being laid-off from my job multiple times. Amongst other things, being able to reframe my situation has really helped me. My job title or the company I work for in the bigger picture will be unimportant. Within the span of one year, our local Muslim community lost two of its most senior and active members in the Bay Area. What positions they held, the cars they drove or the houses they lived in are rarely the things they are remembered for. The death of anyone close, especially when it comes as a total surprise, catches us off guard. What struck me at one funeral was that this individual was a healthy person who I used to play tennis with on weekends. He had an active life and within twenty-four hours of his death we were at the cemetery burying him. However, what I remember about him is his smile and generosity, especially at charitable fund-raisers. And I remember his courage...

On the night of Halloween, he and his family were preparing to come to the mosque (Muslims do not celebrate this event). There was a knock on the door and he opened it only to be faced by costumed men with guns. Not the usual "trick-or-treaters"! They bound and gagged the family and then robbed them. Fortunately, there was no personal harm inflicted other than the violation of safety within their home. Along with our other weekend sports warriors, we played tennis with him the following morning. I would learn about this event later and was never able to ask him how he had the courage, after being robbed at gunpoint the night before, to just go on with life as usual and not be afraid.

Living a life of purpose means we don't get derailed by the detours of life. This is easier said than done, but very powerful when we can do it.

Moses, Mission, and Miracle

According to a scholar's narration, Moses was one time looking for firewood to keep his pregnant wife warm. While searching, he found and was given something else: Prophethood. His first assignment was to go immediately to the Pharaoh and warn him to believe in God or face the consequences. His inner concern was who would look after his wife if he were to go away but as a Prophet, his mission in life was clear.

To relieve his anxiety, God commanded Moses to strike a rock with his staff. When he did this, the rock shattered and there was another rock inside. This, too, he was asked to strike and found another rock, which again he struck. In it, he found an insect like creature with a green leaf in its mouth. Moses then thought to himself that if God can provide for his creation in the most remote and unlikely places, then He would provide for his wife and unborn child. Moses received the message and started his assignment immediately. This and other examples of who feeds the baby for nine months in the womb all lead us to realize that God provides sustenance through His infinite means. One of God's attributes is that He is "*Ar-Razzaq*," the sustainer. He sustains His creation providing both physical and spiritual sustenance.

Sometimes, when we lose our jobs or we have a financial hardship, we can get depressed. Our concern is that we lost our job, a paycheck and our sustenance. We think the job is the ultimate source rather than a channel or means through which we get our sustenance.

This is not to say money is not important. After all, who doesn't need or like money? Just as blood circulation keeps the body alive, the money supply keeps the world we live in going. However, is the pursuit of life, liberty and the purchase of happiness a realistic and meaningful goal? Will that new monster home or truck give you the peace of mind you are looking for? In the developed world, the link between income and happiness is surprisingly weak. Once an individual or family can afford the necessities of life, the incremental income does not bring a proportional amount of joy.

There are many examples of those who are materially rich yet spiritually impoverished. In that case being materially poor is not a bad thing, especially if one is spiritually rich and one can live an honorable life. How pitiful the life of this world! Even if you are prosperous in one aspect you are sure to be miserable in another. Maybe it is health, wealth or some other aspect of life. If one set of problems go away, others replace it. Finally, when everything may seem to be going well, life's journey may have come to an end.

We are caught up and tethered to the material treadmill of life; we sometime forget why we started in the first place. We become so consumed by wanting what we do not have—or need—we forget contentment for what we do have. The more we possess, the more possessed we become...and the more anxious that we may lose it all.

It is surprising to hear that some of those people who are in miserable conditions like those living in slums or the squalor of Calcutta are happier than we imagine. A survey commissioned by the think tank Demos and published in *The Sunday Times*, placed Bangladesh, one of the poorest nations on the planet, at the top of the list of nations with the happiest people alive. Now that is something to ponder! Perhaps those who curb their desires are more content than those with large bank balances. The larger the aspiration gap, the greater the discontent.

Charitable action is also self-healing. The process of giving not only money but also time, attention and love to those in need helps to nurture the self. When you stop comparing yourself to others and are content with who you are and how God has made you, you will not be thrown off track. Earn enough to sustain you and your family. After that, the extra money makes little difference in contentment. Next time you are in the store, ask yourself, "Do I really need this? Is there an alternative? Will this bring inner joy to me and those around me? Is it worth my labor? How long will this joy last?" The question for us is not how can I be happier but how can I accept who I am with what I have been given and how can I give the best of what I have? Happiness lies in not having what you want, but in wanting what you have. If you are content, then you are not trying to achieve someone else's goals.

PURPOSE AND PERSPECTIVE

Perspective is a powerful tool. Two men look from behind bars, one sees the mud the other stars. What makes one see the proverbial glass always half empty and the other half full? You can live your life seeing and feeling abundance. Abundance is not just an excess of material possessions but a state of mind.

In his prayer, Prophet Muhammad said, "O God I seek refuge in you from disbelief and I seek refuge in you from being overwhelmed by debt and men." Live a life of abundance, for many of us it is a choice. Every life has an end towards which we work. A large part of it is spent in accumulating things.

RUMI AND REFRAMING

My favorite poems and stories about reframing and looking at things from a different viewpoint are from the famous sage and poet, Jalal al-Din Rumi.

"What do you really possess? And what have you gained in this life? What pearls have you brought from the depths of the sea? On the day of death, your physical senses will vanish. Do you have the spiritual light to illuminate your heart? What just fills your eyes in the grave? Will your grave shine brightly?" (Masnavi II 939-941)

Reframing is a powerful tool once your purpose in life is clear...

There was once a mule that had been worked very hard by his master. It was poorly fed and treated. Utterly exhausted from his lifetime of labor, beatings, and lack of respect and rewards; the mule had given up.

One day, the master of the royal stables saw the condition of the mule and took pity on him. He was brought in and given the same royal treatment as the Sultan's stallions. Clean grounds, fresh water to drink and the best food one could ask for. He was groomed, rubbed and spoken to with encouraging words. As a result of this same treatment, the Arab horses stabled with the mule were strong and handsome, the envy of every eye.

The mule, seeing their wonderful condition, lifted his head and asked God, "Lord, am I not your creation, too? I know I am a mule, but why am I so lean and wretched, covered with sores? I wish to die each night, my Lord. Why am I so sad, whereas these steeds are so happy?"

A few days later, war started and the Sultan's stallions were engaged in battle. It was a bloody war, and many of them returned from the battlefield with wounds and gashes. As the surgeons extracted the arrows and spears, the horses cried out in pain and agony. The mule once again lifted his head and said, "Oh, God! I am content with my condition. I would rather be a poor mule than a strong stallion. I enjoy my spiritual food and have no desire for the plentiful food. I can endure my condition over the hideous wounds." No matter how hard our lot in life and despite how glamorous the lives of others may appear, our reality may be much better. Once the donkey knew his role in life, his true purpose, he did not need to compare himself to the Sultan's stallions.

In contemporary times, I can think of no better example than the late Princess Diana who outwardly had a fairy tale marriage, beauty, and grace. Yet, as her memoirs revealed later, she was not only someone who was miserable and felt imprisoned in the royal household but she also had made several attempts to take her own life.

We all face situations where anxiety and depression can strike us. The Prophet Muhammad offered the best antidote to alleviate these sentiments. When he woke up each day, he would start by saying "O, God! I seek refuge in you from anxiety and depression."

Anxiety is to the mind and heart what cancer is to the body. It is a silent killer. Although uncertainty is part of life, too much of it makes it a destructive behavior. Becoming a prisoner of the past, a hostage of the present or a captive of the future is no way to live. It is interesting that when you ask how people are doing a common response is "hanging in there." We are supposed to live life to its fullest, not be hanging or falling.

One time a group of people wanted to test the Caliph Ali. He was the fourth of the righteous Caliphs who ruled the Muslim lands after the death of the Prophet Muhammad. He was known to be a wise man. They asked him, "What is the strongest thing that God created?" His reply? Mountains are the obvious strong creation with their age, height and breadth. But metal can cut down a mountain, therefore metal must be stronger. But fire can melt down metal, therefore fire must be stronger. But a fire can be put out with water, therefore water must be stronger. But clouds carry the water, therefore clouds must be stronger. But wind directs the clouds, therefore wind must be stronger. But the son of Adam (humankind) is not moved by the wind, therefore man must be stronger. But intoxicants can dominate a man, therefore intoxicants must be stronger. But sleep erases the symptoms of intoxication, therefore sleep must be stronger. But...anxiety prevents sleep, therefore anxiety is the strongest thing God created!

There you have it, a chain of strong elements; however, even the strongest can be overcome by something else. Of course, this can be a continuing story as anxiety, too, can be overcome by God's mercy and compassion, so God is ultimately the strongest. If our purpose aligns with His, we as humans can be in total harmony.

Going back to the narrative of the Prophet, not only did he seek refuge from anxiety but also from the state of grief and depression. If depression is bad enough, things can deteriorate from there. As we know, some people unfortunately commit suicide. How do we overcome these silent-killers? One of the major ways is by living a purposeful life. Purpose not only gives mission and meaning, it gives hope. Living on purpose is liberating in all aspects. Live that way, live free. People who have purpose are also resilient and that is what the following section discusses.

O Lord Teach Me The Ways of Contentment

A Poem by HEATHER K. BROWNE

O Lord teach me the ways of contentment
To be satisfied with my blessings
The joy of a child's embrace
The warmth of my love's gaze
The sweetness of a bird's song
The fragrance of a flower's bloom

> O Lord teach me the ways of contentment
> To quiet my greedy spirit
> The allure of wealth
> The temptation of self-indulgence
> The excitement of victory
> The anticipation of more

O Lord teach me the ways of contentment
To rely on You for happiness
The wisdom of Your will
The fullness of Your bounty
The awesomeness of Your power
The certainty of Your mercy

BUILDING RESILIENCY

Think of a time when you suddenly experienced a loss or change in your life. Pause, think and write down that event. What did you do? What helped you? What can you learn from it? What can you do now to move forward?

Whether going through a divorce, loss of a job, death, serious illness or other difficult times; it can be a bumpy, unpredictable emotional roller coaster ride. Many times it is hard to escape grief. The roller coaster ride down starts with feelings of shock, denial, anger, uncertainty, grieving and the ride up with reflection, finding new strengths, taking responsibility and re-committing to a new future. Everyone's ride will be different and some people will be on this ride longer than they planned. While some parts of the ride may be unpredictable there are steps you can take to better manage your reaction to the peaks and valleys you'll experience. Being resilient is one of them.

What enables people to deal with hardship? It involves resilience, an ongoing process that requires time and effort and engages people in taking a number of steps. Resilience is "bouncing back" from difficult experiences.

Resilience is the process of adapting in the face of adversity. It is the renewable capacity within us to heal, regenerate and grow from our experience. It is the ability to bounce back and requires an optimistic view of the future. This is not something we are necessarily born with. It is an attitude and behavior that can be developed. Remember, adversity is fleeting not forever. Rather than blaming others or yourself, taking responsibility for things that you can grow from is important. You can't change the wind but you can adjust your sails.

Some people write about their deepest thoughts and feelings related to trauma or other stressful events in their life. Meditation and spiritual practices help some people build connections and restore hope. The key is to identify ways that are likely to work well for you as part of your own personal strategy for fostering resilience.

YOUR BODY, YOUR MIND

According to a survey done in the UK, only three percent of the women were happy with their bodies. Other numbers show the vast majority of women are consumed about their size or shape. Many of them said their body image makes them feel depressed. What is the barometer by which these women measure their happiness? By an overwhelming margin it is the celebrities, who by definition do not have "normal" lives. There is plenty of research which shows how women seeing attractive models for a few minutes began to view their own bodies more negatively. Some magazines dedicate issues to the most beautiful men or women of our time. What makes their top ten or fifty list the standard by which we should all compare ourselves? In fact, it's not unlikely the pictures we are judging ourselves on are air-brushed, touched-up perfection courtesy of graphic artists and plastic surgery. Next time you are at work, a social gathering or standing in line at the grocery store, look around you. What percentage of those people are really handsome or beautiful? The very idea is subjective to begin with. Some would say you know beauty when you see it. Define it any way you want, if you look at a cross section of society, you will find the usual bell curve distribution. Most people look "average" and then there will be a few who are endowed with the gift of beauty and some who may have other qualities.

Think about it, our bodies and looks are given to us by our

Creator. Yet our modern culture has become obsessed with the outer beauty and lost all touch with inner beauty. The number of makeovers includes lifts, reductions, tummy tucks, face-lifts and other items too embarrassing to mention here. It is not a crime to grow old gracefully. People have become obsessed with looking young. Once again, our aging media idols lead the way, but we don't have to follow them

The Qur'an says, "Surely We created people of the best stature" (95:4), yet we have become possessed to change creation. Besides the physical scars and pains of going through surgery, little attention is given to the fact that people who have low self-esteem will not automatically start feeling better about themselves in the long run.

One of my favorite quotes from Rumi on this subject is "Your physical attributes, like your body, are merely borrowed. Do not set your heart on them, for they are transient and only last for an hour. Your spirit by contrast is eternal; your body is on the earth, like a lamp, but its light comes from that everlasting source from above." (Masnavi IV 1840-1842)

One of the divine attributes of God is "Al-Musawwir", the shaper of beauty. He is the One who is the perfect artist, who gives everything the most unique and beautiful form, both visible and hidden. Each and every creation of God is in his infinite wisdom. Let us discover our inner and outer beauty that we have been endowed with and accept it, using it in the best way.

ATTITUDE OF GRATITUDE

The Chinese symbol for the word 'crisis' is a composite of the symbol for "danger" and "opportunity". Crisis can be a dangerous time but also a time to look for new opportunities. How then, can you move forward in a time of crisis?

Believing and visualizing success is an essential factor. People from all walks of life, from sports icons to scientists, visualize their dreams and then plan and take action. It is very important to write down (even if it is a on a single sheet of paper) your vision, your goals and tasks. These will be referred to in the planning principle of the following chapter. Although prayers contain positive affirmations, they can be supplemented with your internal and external dialogue. You must project confidence no matter what obstacles you are facing. This doesn't mean projecting a Pollyanna and unreal "life is wonderful" demeanor but really believing what you say. Otherwise, your real self will show through.

For some of us projecting an aura of confidence may seem unreal. Think for a minute. Who are the kind of people you like being around? The "cheerful regardless of my circumstances" type or the "depressed, life is miserable" type? Unless you're in a manic depression, my hope is that you chose the former. Now, pause again and think what kind of a person are you like to be around? The constant complainer, fault-finder? Or the "life is good, thank you, God" type? If it's the former, the bad news is you may not be fun to be around! Although we all have certain genetic dispositions, attitude and the resulting behavior is something that can be learnt and changed. Watch your thoughts as they become your words, watch your words as they become your actions, and watch your actions as they become your habits. It's your choice who you want to be. The following example of Shiraz and the dove shows gratitude in action.

SHIRAZ AND THE DOVE: GRATITUDE AND PURPOSE

There once lived a farmer by the name of Shiraz, who enjoyed the good life. Plenty of harvest and no worries. As happens in good times he did not remember or thank God for his blessings. One year, the lands were overcome with drought and Shiraz went from worry to despair. "How could this happen to me?" was his response and he became resentful to God for his misfortune.

One hot day, Shiraz decided to head to town looking for work. On the journey, he cast his eyes on a dove that was limping along the ground with an injured wing. In spite of the pain, the bird praised God and thanked Him. He was very astonished that the small creature was badly injured yet was showing thankfulness to God and praising Him over and over. Shiraz became curious and asked the dove why she was thanking God.

The bird replied to Shiraz by saying, "Oh, man! Why shouldn't I be thankful? I have good health and despite my condition, I provide for my family. He has showered His mercy on me and comforted me at times of need. He allows me to get up each day, breathe the air and fly over the seas, safely returning to a loving family. I have not experienced real distress and so not one or two broken wings can think of coming close to the limitless blessings and favors I have received from God." The dove then kneeled on the other wing and said, "Now, with God's help as in the past, this injury on my wing will pass by."

Shiraz was flabbergasted and reflected on his own life, just as we should. How many blessings we see and how little gratitude we show! At times of hardship, do we become more patient or spiteful? Shiraz was ashamed of his actions and repented. He learnt a valuable lesson from a dove and spent the rest of his life in obedience to his Creator and Sustainer.

HOPE AND FAITH

"*I claim to be no more than an average person with less than average ability. I have not the shadow of doubt that any man or woman can achieve what I have, if he or she would make the same effort and cultivate the same hope and faith.*" Mahatma Gandhi

Popping Bubbles

A Poem by Rym Aoudia

On a grassy field
Little mouths blew
Bubbles so huge
That floated in the air
Chuckling
Giggling
Little feet ran
Chasing the bubbles
Popping them all

    On a bench I sat
    Watching it all
    Envying their happiness
    Envying the joy
    But deep down I knew
    The wisdom of it all

P and *R*
    O and *B*
  L and *E*
  M and *S*
Scattered problems
In every corner
Some ready to leap
Some already leapt
With teeth so sharp
Scarring my life
So full of strife
More bubbles blown
Huge but light
No matter the size

All did pop
Yes I knew
The wisdom of it all

Like bubbles
Problems appear
They look so big
But hollow from within
Eventually they pop
Oh yes I knew
The wisdom of it all

Allah and His Prophet
Taught us all
That life is so small
Of a few years or so
It'll pop
It'll disappear

Oh yes
Bring endurance on
Oh yes
Call patience over

I kicked off my shoes
Stepped on the grass
Chuckling
Giggling
With the little ones
Popping the bubbles

Chapter 5

PROACTIVE PLANNING

Do you know of anyone who, at some point in his or her life, has not been touched by grief, tragedy or loss? It could be a terminal illness, an accident, death of a loved one, failing an important exam or a business failure. Their career had a meteoric growth and then a crash landing. It is hard to put into words what those who suffer loss go through, a sense of utter despair, emptiness and a numbing of the senses. It can become so intense one questions the meaning of life. Some people are unable to come to terms with loss, some fall victims to depression, others to suicide. Once you recover from the initial shock, there comes a point of acceptance. This is a stage where we can go from being reactive to proactive and that is what this chapter is about.

Being proactive means not only anticipating but working to shape the future. Rather than reacting to events, it means taking charge where ever possible. Being proactive is strongly linked to planning. Vision is a part of planning. One of my favorite stories which illustrate its importance is the following:

One day the donkey said to the camel, "Why is it that God has honored you in His book and said, 'Look at the camel and how We made him.' And yet when He speaks about me, He says, 'The worst of voices is the donkey's voice' and He says, 'The likeness of the ass carrying books'. And He also gave honor to the camel of Prophet Salih. Why is that you have such a high place with God and I have such a low place?"

The camel replied, "Because all you do is look down at your own feet and I look up as far as my eye can see. My vision is vast, I see the horizon and I don't stumble in my path. I will move with speed and effort if somebody sings to me. You move only when you are beaten with a stick."

So far we have covered three principles of overcoming the challenges of life: Prayer, Patience and Purpose. Being grounded in faith, praying and being patient provide an unmovable foundation to life. Once you have identified your purpose, you have a target to aim for. Now we focus on action with preparation, which results in planning. Becoming proactive instead of being reactive makes you persist in what you have planned and enables you to pursue it with passion.

There's a saying that a poor plan is better than no plan. We live in a world where we plan everything in our lives with Day Timers and PDA's (Personal Digital Assistants). Vacations are planned, marriages are planned but we give little attention to the plan of life. If we lose our job then we must find a place and dedicate time for the search. If we find our children are not doing well in school or having other problems, we have to present them more time.

No matter what challenges we face in life, knowledge and planning become necessary. Also, the bigger the crisis, the greater the planning required. There is a deluge of information available about defining a vision, mission and goals—all part of the planning process. Not only do organizations and executives need to do this but individuals must also.

Once you have identified your goals, you need to do a balance sheet check of your assets and liabilities. What are the strengths you can leverage, what are the weaknesses in terms of skills or other things you need to succeed? Are these skills you can learn yourself or are there people you need on your team?

Creating a plan requires identifying what needs to be done and determining how it will be done. Again, there is much information available on this. Planning as an exercise helps to clarify thought. By putting it on paper and having others review it, gives it clarity. As with any plan, it needs to be revisited and updated with time. Any book on goals will tell you they should be SMART: Specific, Measurable, Achievable, Realistic and Tangible

Remember, your goals should be your own and something you believe in. Have goals for different aspects of your life such as faith and family, career and community, health and education. Goals should be positive and motivating. Your mission may be to Mars but what are the steps you need to get there? Get out of bed, get over fear of heights, build a rocket, etc.

Part of planning means looking at options. The creative process means brainstorming options and then coming up with criteria by which you decide what you want to go after. Having one option is not a good place to start. Sooner rather than later, you or somebody else will ask, "Did you try this?" and you will wish you'd given it thought.

Remember, no one gets up in the morning and says today I am going to be patient, or I am going to be proactive or passionate. Well…maybe not the last one, but you get the picture. Being proactive means taking action before crisis happens. It is almost a guarantee that the more challenges you face in life, the more your existing family relations will come under stress.

PROACTIVE PLANNING: WHEN I PRACTICE IT, IT DOES WORK!

I am sure most of us plan for journeys to various degrees. The longer the journey, the more planning we have to do. The greatest journey I undertook was going for the pilgrimage to Mecca for *Hajj*. I did this in pre-Internet times when there was little information on-line at my fingertips about the duty which all Muslims must do once in a lifetime if they are physically and financially able.

My planning included reading and researching the experiences of friends and people who had recently done their *Hajj*. I also researched and planned the provisions to take with us, including the clothes needed for the pilgrimage. For men, they must wear two unstitched, white pieces of cloth. Women may wear what they please as long as it covers them modestly and most prefer to also wear white. My wife and I had decided to leave our children with my mother and sister in England. My wife would leave early so the children would become used to my family there. When it came for my turn to leave, a friend of mine who had gone on the *Hajj* before dropped me off at San Francisco Airport. On the way, he reset my expectations and made them so low that I felt as long as I did not expect or compare the trip to life in the US, things could only be better. During *Hajj*, people do become lost there in a sea of millions of pilgrims. One of the best decisions I made was to take my favorite multi-colored umbrella with us. This way, after any prayer, we could identify not only a meeting point but also easily identify each other.

The rites of the pilgrimage last over five days and cover the tradition of the Prophet Abraham. It requires a presence at different days and times in Mecca and three adjoining cities/lands. The central theme of Hajj is the presence of all the three million plus pilgrims in the land of Arafat. Fail to make it there at the prescribed time and the *Hajj* is void. Break a smaller rule and compensation has to be made in the form of a sacrifice. One of the major events that not only the Pilgrims but all Muslims do in the days after Arafat is a sacrifice commemorating the sacrifice the Prophet Abraham made.

However, even with the best of plans, I did make mistakes. Some of them were made during the rituals of the pilgrimage itself. As I discovered them, I took corrective measures, which are permitted. Others, I had to live with. Walking without shoes (which is the Muslim practice when being in mosques and sacred places) on the marble especially during the walk between the hills of Safa and Marwa took a toll on my feet.

Obviously, not all "journeys" are once in a lifetime events. However, a plan still helps. One of the most invaluable things I learned about being unemployed is the importance of staying busy and carrying on with routines the best you can. For me this has paid dividends. Getting up for prayers and dropping the children in the morning has forced me to get up and stay up. Finding places like libraries or job centers has allowed me to have a place to go to. It has provided an invaluable cushion spouses need so we have space to do our respective work

Making a plan to call past contacts, going to networking events and, yes, picking up the dreaded phone to make calls have all been part of the grand plan. Not being afraid to let others know you need work, without sounding desperate has been invaluable.

Making small corrections as I go along has also helped. For example, I am very open with my family and provided them with daily updates about my job hunt. It soon became annoying when my son would ask each day if I had landed a job. I learned it was better to provide updates once a week so as not to be under constant scrutiny from the family. We all have different personality types, some much more structured than others, but being proactive and planning ahead are invaluable to all of us. Not everything has to be planned to the nth degree; there is joy in being spontaneous, too. However, there are aspects of life that can help with structure. Be like the camel: have a vast vision, see the horizon, be proactive and let the stars guide you on your journey of life.

A specific example of planning involves looking for a job. One could go about it in an ad-hoc way or develop a systematic way. The following seven habits helped me in my job search.

Seven Habits of Highly Effective Job Seekers

1.0 Set Goals

   1.1 Use a planner

   1.2 Develop a Business Plan

   1.3 Target Specific Companies

   1.4 Open up to new options

   e.g. to new types of jobs, location, position

2. 0 Establish a time and place to do the job search

   2.1 Find a place to go first thing in the morning

   e.g. Library, Outplacement Center

   2.2 Get a library card

3.0 Maximize networking opportunities

   3.1 Use varied networking opportunities

   (Chamber of Commerce, Professional organizations, industry groups, e-mail groups specific to job seekers)

   3.2 Professional affiliations

   3.3 Any time you meet friends/associates

3.4 Get business cards

(www.vistaprint.com: free cards, pay for shipping)

4.0 Have a balanced life

4.1 Allocate time to do community work, chores, fun activities

4.2 Find a passionate hobby and give it time

(avoid boredom and depression)

4.3 Exercise! It improves morale and reduces stress

5.0 Deal with emotions

5.1 It's natural to get angry, feel "why me?"

Need good ways to vent

Listen and agree on common points of arguments

5.2 Discuss Solutions

6.0 Hope for the best, plan for the worst

6.1 The typical job search now takes longer

(6-8+ months is average)

6.2 Need to be patient and hopeful

6.3 Need strong support team of family and friends

6.4 Need a financial plan and budget (expenses vs. income)

6.5 Call lenders and ask to have your payments reduced

7. 0 Have faith and trust in God

We know life is a test. If we do our best, God will take care of the rest. Remember God has power over all things. If you recognize your position in life, make your efforts and then resign to Him in sincerity and total dependence, you will reap many rewards. Returning to God leads to a state of humility. If you are patient, happy about the benefits and look forward to the rewards in the hereafter, you will come out the real winner. Being content gives a peace and stability to life, which cannot be compared with anything.

Nice Theory, Where's the Practice?

To those who are somewhat pessimistic in life or just skeptical about what has been covered, I would like to dedicate this section to you. Let me share with you a saying of the Prophet Muhammad, "Verily God ordered me to keep relations with those that cut me off, to forgive the one who does injustice with me and to give to those who withhold from me."

There is no doubt every category of hardship and tribulation is different. Job loss is different than loss of a loved one, a family dispute is different than a civil dispute, having an allergy is different than a life threatening illness. On top of this, even within one category, no two people's situations will be exactly the same. That is why we as human beings are unique individuals, with unique experiences. However, do not fall victim to thinking "only I know what I am going through." Yes, indeed you and God know uniquely what you are going through but the journey of life has been going on for thousands of years and although humankind has gone through many revolutions from the industrial to the information, the basics of human nature have not. We can learn not only from the past but also from the present and hope for a better understanding of the future.

Look at the example of marriage and conflicts that arise from friction caused by in-laws. Is this something unique to one group of people or culture? Actually it is a common denominator across cultures. There are many variations on it, but the fundamentals do not change. Protective mother-in-law, naive daughter-in-law and so forth. Remember most mother-in-laws were daughter-in-laws at one time, yet very few become the role model mother-in-laws. This is not to pick on mother-in-laws; the issue may be with another member of the family.

No two people's situation will be the same, but there are things that we can all do that help alleviate the suffering. No matter how bad your situation, not only could things be worse, there are so many people out there whose situation is worse. Have hope, do what you can and leave your affairs with God. Go through the worst-case scenario and once you're done, write it down and put it in a safe place.

In most cases, with time and reflection, you can reframe the same event as a minor glitch. Many of the material problems or family issues are petty compared to our higher purpose in life. You or somebody else will not care about this in an hour, a day, a year from now. Some may keep grudges but, in the end, does this merit your worries and energy or are there better things you could be spending it on? Judge everything in its true value and then put it in its proper place. If you can be content with what God has given you, you will be the richest of people.

God has not created anything or anyone without purpose. You do not have to be rich, famous or powerful to be a person who has self-worth and importance. If you doubt that ask your spouse, children, or other family and sincere friends. The problem for many of us is that we march to the beat of other people's drums. What is your calling in life? Do not think it has to be something glamorous. If you break down the life of most people, it is composed of doing what may be perceived as monotonous things, which we have to persevere with.

If you have faith to live by, safe shelter to live under, you are able-bodied, have family and friends to find comfort in, food to eat and clean water to drink, then you are better off than the vast majority of the population on this planet.

Ask yourself, *Do I delay living in the present because of fears and apprehensions about the future or because of hopes of the magical garden beyond the horizon? Do I embitter my present life by mulling over events that occurred in the past?* As an Arab poet said, "The past is lost forever and that which is hoped for is the unseen, so that all you have is the present hour."

The following sections discuss specific ideas that can help put principles into practice.

Lost In Emotion and Finding Support

Every situation, good or bad, comes with emotions. In some cases, our responses will be similar and in other cases, they will be very different. Sometimes, you may be the one riding the highs and lows and at other times it may be you who is offering the emotional support. Regardless, turning to others for comfort, advice and faith is very important. Life can be even better and more fulfilling if we can find ways to endure hardships together. Whatever your challenge or tribulation, you will need a support team to get you there. There is no such thing as being a "lone ranger." Family, sincere friends, well meaning associates and mentors are vital on the mission. Although each provides general support the roles will be different. However, one thing is for sure—make them your trusted advisors.

To manage difficult times in life creatively, one of the most important things a family can do is to help reframe the situation. Although fear, uncertainty and doubt may come into play, the sooner we can move away from the initial shock or sense of despair and get to the point of acceptance, the quicker we can become a part of he solution as opposed to the problem. Open communication and dialogue, including venting emotions, is a part of the healing process. Then there is a need to focus on how they can work together to meet the challenges they face.

Unless you are trying to be of help to others who are going through tough times, be around positive people as much as you can. Attitude is contagious. Your support group should include someone who can be a mentor and people who believe in you.

Having faced long term unemployment, one thing I can say assuredly is the support of my family and a handful of sincere friends who regularly checked in with us and gave us the moral boost to ride this roller coaster. Everyone's role may be a little different but the key thing is knowing there are people out there that care for you. If someone has been through that situation, illness or experience, it assists in the support process as you realize you are nor alone. A support group gives you the strength and confidence to go forward in life.

Talking to someone who is a non-judgmental, good listener while you are going through a time of distress, is very important. In many cases, they become an empathic ear and a helping hand. They may or may not be able to give you advice, but that is secondary. Being able to vent not only allows you to discharge some of the negative energy but it also allows you to bring your thoughts and feelings together and make sense of them. Both talking about and listening to shared fears and anxieties helps the healing process. Can you change the situation and see some good in it? Is there some way you could have contributed to the problem? If so, learn from it, accept responsibility and move on.

Not every situation can be resolved through social support and avoidance of problems. Some may warrant confrontation, where you have to fight for what you want or need. Others may mean an amicable separation. Remember though, holding a grudge has a boomerang effect. The greater your resentments, the more they come back towards you. If grudges are held, they become barriers in the healing process.

There are indeed situations where you have been wronged. No one should accept physical or verbal abuse. If somebody makes defamatory comments to you, the natural response is to defend yourself, yet in many cases it will only escalate the situation.

Every situation and individual is different. In the end, you must evaluate what the relationship means to you. The more important the relationship, the greater the need to try and resolve it in some manner. Forgiveness and forbearance—if you have the courage to do them—are very powerful for healing. The Qur'an says, "And when they are angry they forgive" (42:37) and, "When the foolish address them (with bad words) they reply back with mild words of gentleness." (25:63) This reference is to the believers.

Remember, tribulations and trials have many benefits. They make us aware of our well being, especially when we see how good our life is compared to many others. "*When does gold ore become gold? When it is put through a process of fire. So the human being during the training becomes as pure gold through suffering. It is the burning away of the dross.*" (Bhai Sahib) Tribulations prevent us from arrogance, evil, pride and, yes, even tyranny. If we are forgiving and forbearing, giving and compassionate to those who wrong us, it releases us from the straightjacket of revenge, which ties us into knots. Taking the higher moral ground frees us from looking for revenge.

Just as nature is full of positive and negative charges, mood swings, emotional highs and lows are a natural byproduct of who we are as human beings. Although we cannot be in total control of our moods, we do not have to become slaves to them either. Moods change not only from day to day but many times within the same day as you ride the emotional roller coaster. The key thing is not to let the negative emotions spill over and affect those we live, work or associate with. The funny thing about emotions, especially when we are at a low or a high, is that they may not reflect the true situation. Given time to pause, reflect, get distracted, you may see the humor or other positive perspective.

An example.

One day I was about to drop my teenage daughter off at school. In the usual mad rush, we discovered as we got close to school that she forgot to wear her shoes. My first reaction was not "how funny". I was frustrated and wondered how could anyone leave the house and forget their shoes? I was angry and couldn't stop thinking about the fact I would have to drive ten miles back home to get the shoes and in the process become even later. But I made another choice and began to laugh with my daughter—a memory sweetened by joy to be looked back on with delight. If it is moody people you are dealing with, being understanding and patient can help. That is the way I view it; as long as these are not repeat offenses and I care about the relationship, it is something I can choose to overlook. How about you?

THE ART OF MARRIAGE:
PLANNING THE MARRIAGE, NOT THE WEDDING

I am always amazed at how so much time is spent in planning for marriages, not only months but sometimes years. So much attention is paid to the decorations, the wedding dress, and the cake. And yet, sadly, more than half of these marriages end up in divorce. Many of them do not make it past even the first few months or years. Again, marriage is an important social institution. We spend so much time planning for one day, yet so little for the life that lies ahead. We spend four or more years going to college, yet we are so unprepared to address working life. We spend a few days on this earth and are so unprepared for life's real journey ahead.

Marriage humor says that in the first year, the man speaks and the woman listens. In the second year, the woman speaks and the man listens. In the third year, they both speak and the neighbors listen.

It is a sad reality that marriage has become either so romanticized as to be unreal or made so much fun of that it's becoming a dying institution. The divorce rate and the horror stories do not help. However, marriage is a pillar of stability and happiness for many people. There is plenty of evidence which shows that, to enhance happiness, one should find God, get married, stay married, have children, keep up with relatives and friends and be content with what you have. A great read on this subject is "The Case for Marriage - Why Married People Are Happier, Healthier and Better Off Financially." People who have faith have meaning and purpose in life. When they are faced with adversity, they are able to draw on a spiritual reservoir of healing and support. Married people are consistently happier than singles.

Are all marriages "made in heaven"? I am not going to touch that but first know that every marriage will face different trials. Just as adversity in other aspects of life can strengthen you, so can it in marriage if handled properly. No issue is so complex it cannot be solved or so trivial it cannot be overlooked. With prayers and sincere hearts you can weather any storm. What are some of the secrets of happy couples and how they cultivate their relationships? Read the following.

Seven Secrets of Successful Marriage

There are many things that make a marriage successful. From a principles standpoint, they cover things like having common faith, showing forgiveness, putting family first, having fun, being flexible, and many more. Another category would be being committed to each other, accepting each other for who we are and encouraging each other with good communication. Communication which include listening, acknowledging, showing respect and trust are fundamental. When you say "I understand you" or in conflict situations you say "maybe you're right" or "please forgive me", they go a long way in strengthening family bonds. Although I do not think anyone would disagree with the above, in the end every marriage needs a catalyst to help it along. The following secrets are something that I have experienced and would like to share.

1. Take a timeout with each other everyday. This could be a walk around the block, which we find can be very therapeutic. On a good day we can not only get exercise but share experiences and solve problems. On a bad day, we create more problems, but fortunately the good outweighs the bad. Other ways of spending time together could be a family meeting (which is not always the most popular event if you have teenagers); it's a way to talk about your day, vent a frustration, share good news or solve a problem. If you're still looking for more ideas, try helping with the dishes or something that can be done in tandem.

2. Develop and maintain a strong social support network of family and friends. All relationships have to be nurtured. From spouse to parents, in-laws, siblings and close friends. Being there as a moral and other support not only helps strengthen these bonds, but also is

rewarding spiritually. I could not have imagined having gone through three years of unemployment with out my faith, family and friends. In-law issues are common across cultures. There are some inherent issues which exist, for example the tug of war between the mother-in-law and daughter-in-law. Although some adjustments do take place with time, others like skepticism may not. Issues of supporting dependent parents are common. I do not have a silver-bullet for any of these issues. Be as just as you can with all parties and my favorite is "do unto others...". A strong network works to the benefit of all, in a few words it says "Count on me, I'll be there."

3. Discuss and decide the various roles each spouse and later family member will take. In any organization, whether it is family or corporation, decisions have to be made. Consensus works up to a point, but there will always be sticky issues. eg it only took us about four years to agree on a sofa we could both live with. Decide the roles each spouse will play. For example, I am the CEO (Chief Executive Officer), my wife is the COO (Chief Operating Officer), my son is the CJO, (Chief Janitorial Officer, responsible for putting out the garbage), and all three children are Co-CEOs (Chief Entertainment Officers). Who is the Chief Financial Officer? Well we have out-sourced that position!

4. Learn to become content. This I feel is a life-long process. We all know about not comparing ourselves with the Jones's over material things but it goes a lot further. If we are annoyed with our spouse, letting them know and comparing them to someone else is unlikely to help the relationship. You or your spouse will never measure up to someone else's image. Accepting each other and then later on with children and other family members is an invaluable asset. I am not

saying it is easy. There are too many times my wife or I have gotten our child's report card or rebuked them on some bad behavior by comparing them with their peers. The Prophet Muhammad said the greatest richness is being content. Once you learn to become content, it gives a peace of mind that cannot be purchased at any price. At the other extreme, this is not an excuse to become complacent over our weaknesses.

5. Give gifts. Gifts can be material, but they don't always have to be. When I travel on business, I usually make it a point to get something for each family member. If we are invited for dinner, it is nice to take a gift for our hosts. Sometimes, a gift can be something as small as a smile, a hug, an encouraging word or a word of appreciation. We all know about saying "thank you" and "I love you", but with time they either wear off or we start taking things for granted. There are times when I have said something and later thought I may have hurt someone's feelings. A little call is all it takes to mend or build the relationship. These little gifts show that we respect, honor and accept those around us. I would not trade the world for the hug that I get from my four year old daughter when she comes running to me after a long day's work and says, "I missed you and I love you!" Give a smile, give a hug...all gifts are truly precious.

6. Be committed for life. Marriage, like a car, needs on-going maintenance. Only for this one the maintenance has to be done by us. Marriage is a part of the roller coaster ride, so when we commit to "for better or for worse", we have to sincerely mean it and apply it. I am not shouting conspiracy theories here, but there are many external factors vying to derail marriage. Television and billboard images, the daytime and reality shows create unreal expectations about marriage.

If, as in any tradition, we commit ourselves to leading chaste and respectable lives by not flirting, or being in situations where we can become vulnerable, that is one more way we can keep our marriages intact.

7. Always look to continue to improve as a spouse, parent or whatever the relationship is. Every once in a while change your routines. What worked in the first few years of marriage may not work later. Successful couples grow with each other. Create freshness so you adapt with time. In our case, this means always being on the look out to learn whether it be from books or examples of others and sharing with each other. No matter how familiar the subject, I feel there is always something I can and do learn.

SURVIVING AND THRIVING IN 20+ YEARS OF MARRIAGE: A CASE STUDY OF THE MOHAMMED FAMILY

Rather than just talk about what makes other couples and marriages succeed, I was asked to bring the voice of my wife and family into the book. This is a transcript of the Mohammed family meeting with special attention given to what's allowed us to be just as crazy as any other family and still survive.

THE CAST OF CHARACTERS

Nasreen Mohammed: 40+ homemaker and chief child-care and cooking officer

Nasir: 18-yr-old college student

Aliyah: 14-yr-old middle school student

Nadia: 4-yr-old imaginary student

Javed Mohammed: 44-yr-old still trying to figure out what to do for next 20 years

Javed: So what makes our marriage and family tick?

Nasreen: It's about communication, talking to each other, not hiding things, being open, not lying, even if it's writing a book, hint hint.

Javed: Technically, I didn't lie; I just didn't confirm that I was working on it.

Nasreen: You know the rule that I use to have for the older kids? If you tell the truth, you won't get in trouble. If you chose to lie you get a little dose of chilies in your mouth.

Javed: Well, I am glad you don't have that rule anymore

Nasir: So why did I get the chilies?

Nasreen: Because you spilled milk in the back of the car and denied it.

Nasir: So how do you know it was milk?

Nasreen: Well, with a smell like that after one week, it was obviously not my perfume and remember, I am a great detective

Nasir: I say it was your bad driving that spilled the milk.

Javed: OK, folks we're getting off track here. What are the things that help us as a family or this marriage tick?

Aliyah: You, Dad, never go to sleep angry (little does she know   ).

Nadia: Daddy, hit Nasir-bhai, he's being mean to me (Nadia has a box of Trix.)

Nasreen: Life is full of Trix and politics. Life is colorful just like this cereal. Every day is a different color

Javed: Wow, I didn't realize a box of cereal could be so inspiring and make you philosophical!

Nasir: Life is like a chili, it's hot from beginning to end. Actually, it's like a drama from beginning to end.

Aliyah: Wow, looks like the chilies are making you philosophical

Nasreen: Life is running around. When the baby is born you're running around finding a name, looking for clothes. At the end, still running around looking for a coffin and grave.

Aliyah: Life is about mutual respect.

Nadia: I hate you stupid!

Now Nadia grabs Aliyah and they both fall over the chair.

Family meeting closed.

Even family life can be successful when the whole family is included or when there is humor involved. Having planned time to discuss issues or otherwise plan for the week ahead are great ways to use family meetings.

Jewels For Your Soul

A Poem by ELOQUENCE AN-NUR

My child, there are a few things
You have to know before I go
For sure, we were very poor
When you were first born.

> I cried, as I prayed, at times
> Because we had such a rough ride
> Yet, God never cast us aside
> And we weathered the tide.

When all of our resources had been spent
And there was no money to be lent
Mommy prayed for the rent.
Know the money came through heaven sent.

> So, always maintain your pride
> And don't do just anything to make a dime.
> Don't you ever sell your soul
> Because jail and hell are hot as coal.

Remember that we've struggled through many tests
Our much more has followed our much less
So, should your money ever be stressed
You just have faith and know that you are blessed.

> This is your legacy,
> These are my jewels for your soul
> All through our ancestry,
> Our people have had a strength unknown
> Even through poverty,
> We've had riches more than gold

You just have faith and see,
How your dreams will unfold.
You just have faith and see,
How your dreams will unfold.

My child take this advice –
Don't ever let anyone seduce you into vice.
When people start drinking
And they start acting loose
Step aside, be quick to slide

Because you've got great things to produce.
People will act a fool
And the world is very cruel
But, you follow the Golden Rule
Do for others as you would have them do for you.

Though at times you'll be deceived,
You fall down on your knees
And you pray and believe,
You will achieve, you will succeed.

Know that God is never far
Tell Him what He needs to hear;
That it's only Him that you fear
Through your trials God will hold you dear.

These are my jewels for your souls

Chapter 6

PASSIONATE PERSISTENCE

My side of the family is known to be very passionate. I use this word in a larger context. Perhaps it is the spicy food we eat (maybe long ago we were Italian; I don't know what else to attribute it to). I think we all know what passion is. I like to think of passion as the fuel that propels us through the journey called life. As we ride the roller coaster and we hit the low points, it is the passion that keeps us going forward. To be successful, passion and perseverance must come into play.

As success lies in perseverance, let me share the example of the man who was standing by the side of a rock. He looked down and found that due to the continuous lashing of the waves, the rock had worn away. Then he remarked, "Look, the rock is a hard object, while water is so soft. But even if a thing as soft as water acts with perseverance, it can crush an object as hard as a rock into pieces. All the huge quantities of sand found on the sea shores have been produced by this lashing of water against the rocks."

PASSIONATE SOMETIMES AND BEEN KNOWN TO PERSEVERE

It's nice talking about passion and perseverance, but here are some examples I have to share. My own examples of perseverance vary. While at college in Manchester University, I went on a 55 mile charitable walk. The first year I had no idea what it took, did not pace it and was out of steam half way through. The following year I paced it and managed to drag myself to the end. The third year I tried again with my sister on a nice rainy night and again only made it about half way. Another example is while living in Japan, like many of the locals, I attempted to climb Mount Fuji at night so we could see the sunrise. It was a long and tiring journey. No planning, no water, just sticking with it. Seeing old and young people gave me hope to carry on. The view was worth it. It was spectacular to see for the first time lightening at such a high elevation. The sunrise was even more breath taking than words can describe.

Writing, especially books, has not come easy for me. My first book took approximately seven to eight years to write, with two long breaks where I quit on the manuscripts. It was a mid-life crisis and a more educated approach that helped me get through the third (and successful!) attempt with *Gems of Wisdom, Heart of Gold*. To writing, as it was so much work, I said, never again, but September 11, 2001, happened and I was forced to write *Islam 101*. I got laid off from my job shortly thereafter and I have always had in the back of my mind this book in your hands. Yes, even writing this book has been a roller coaster. Finding your passion does not mean waiting to line up all the requirements before doing something. In many instances, it is a case of "Ready, Fire, Aim."

When I was laid off for the second time, I started holding weekly classes for other unemployed people. I was not any more qualified than the rest of my peers, but I had the passion to want to make a difference. When I came back from Hajj, I wrote a mini-booklet to help others who would embark on this journey. When I remodeled my house and survived, I wrote about this experience in another booklet and handed it out to family and friends. In many ways, the writing I have done and continue to do is just for the joy of benefiting others. That is why I consider myself to be the accidental author. It is not that my English, grammar or prose are good; in fact, it is the wonderful job of all the editors that has made it possible, but it is the passion that has helped carry this work through. So many times when I have hit dead-ends in the editorial or the book layout process, it is the passion that has helped us to get through.

There are so many stories of inventors and generals who persevered in the face of obstacles. Pick your role models and never give up. It is okay to regroup, but not to retreat. If we expect that life will be full of tribulations then we will be much better prepared as the roller coaster takes its sudden turns. Passion and perseverance pay off, many times in ways that we do not anticipate. Walk, climb, write, endure and let your passion propel you to pass through the obstacles of life with a perseverance that takes you to your goals. The following is an inspirational story about not only persistence, but also how we can be rewarded.

THE NECKLACE

There once lived a poor and upright man called Aziz in the city of Mecca. At one point in his life, he had not eaten for many days; he was dying of starvation. He looked for work and he looked for food. As he was searching, by chance he came across an expensive necklace. Aziz took the necklace and headed to the mosque. On the way there, he heard a man crying that he had lost a necklace. When Aziz asked him to describe it, he did so perfectly and Aziz returned the necklace without taking a reward. Aziz prayed, "O God, I have given it for You, so compensate me with what is better."

Having exhausted his options in the city and not finding work or food, Aziz headed to the ocean to look for other opportunities. There he took a journey on a small boat. Before long, a storm came and caused the boat to break into pieces. As he clinged to a piece of wood, he was washed ashore onto an island. There he found a mosque where people were praying so he joined them. Later, he was reading the Qur'an and when the natives of the island saw this, they asked him to teach the children and be paid for his services. On another day, they saw Aziz writing and they asked him if he would teach their children to write for an additional salary.

As some time passed, the natives told him an orphan girl whose father was a good man, would be a good spouse. Would he marry her? Aziz agreed and later related the rest of his story...

I married her and saw she was wearing the exact same necklace I had once found when I was dying of hunger. She said her father lost it in Mecca and a man returned it to him. She said her father would always pray for his daughter to become blessed with a husband similar to the honest man. I then informed her that I was that man."

The lesson from Aziz's story is that by being persistent in his search and by staying honest, you will indeed be compensated with something better, either sooner or later.

Twenty-One Practical Ideas
for Riding the Roller coaster of Life

There have been a lot of principles covered so far. Now how can we put them into practice? Again, given that every situation is unique, the following advice is something I hope you can adapt for your own situation.

1. Depend first on God, no matter how big the test. If you begin from the idea that nothing is impossible for Him, then things only get better. Start with a pure and sincere intention and ask through prayers

for God's help. Practice the good that is liked by our Creator and avoid that which He dislikes.

2. Read these lines very slowly and let then sink in:

"If God brought you to it, He will bring you through it." (How do you know if God brought you to that situation? Not so easy to answer, but in life there are things that are beyond one's control).

3. Maintain a strong sense of purpose. If you position your situation in the bigger picture, your perspective will change.

4. Stay upbeat. Look for the positive in spite of the negative. With every problem, there are opportunities. The Qur'an says, "With every hardship there is ease." Rather than thinking about either-or situations, look for win-win principles especially if there are other parties involved.

5. Accept that life is constantly changing, full of turbulence and disruption. The social, political and economic environment is in constant flux. We will encounter turbulence on this journey; adjust your approach...sometimes you ride through it and at other times above it.

6. Learn from life experiences. Read, reflect and discuss with other like-minded people. Take a class, challenge yourself. Take small steps into the direction you want to go.

7. Write down what you are trying to accomplish in life, your purpose and your goals. Make sure they are your goals, as later on you will need the passion to see them through. Do not be a prisoner of the past, live in the present. See what benefits and lessons you can learn from any adversity you face.

8. Tolerate ambiguity. The more flexible you are and the more open-minded about how things turn out, the less you will be hit by setbacks.

9. Build a positive and hopeful outlook on life and yourself. Cut out or minimize the negative news from the media, self-talk and negative people. If you believe you can, look for ways of "how can we" rather than "we can't." No crisis will appear insurmountable.

10. Get creative. Discover new opportunities for self-discovery and to move forward. At this brainstorming stage, no idea is too dumb. Be willing to see diverse perspectives.

11. Consider past successes. To help you with your current situation, think about how you have dealt successfully with past situations. You will be surprised at the reservoir of ideas and energy you had and have. Envision what it will be like having reached a positive outcome.

12. Stay focused and avoid distractions. Once you have identified your goals go with them with a deep sense of mission and desire. Remember, goals should be realistic, measurable and inspirational.

13. Think about what is right in your life, what you have. Sometimes we become pre-occupied with our desires and what we do not have and forget how much we are blessed with.

"This too shall pass." In the midst of a storm or hardship it is difficult to see when your situation will ever get any better. Think about it in the natural world and in our lives, the roller coaster continues its ride.

14. Be Proactive. This means looking ahead and not only anticipating what may happen but being prepared to face it. Granted, we cannot be prepared for every outcome in life but there are sure signs for many things. We just have to open our senses to them. Be prepared to take risks whose consequences you can live with.

15. Look after yourself and those you are responsible for. This involves both the physical and emotional needs. Exercise as well as

communicate often. Don't waste your energy on non-productive, stress-inducing issues you can let go.

16. Develop a support team. This should include your spouse, children, family, friends and a mentor. These are people you can have an open and honest relationship with and share your hopes and fears.

17. Have a giving hand and a caring heart. There are so many people who are in a worse situation than you. Volunteer; help them by providing a hand, a listening ear and a compassionate heart.

18. Remember the Prophetic tradition. In terms of faith, look to those better than you (so they inspire you) and in terms of the material world, look at those below you (as you will see how good your situation is).

19. Be persistent. Setbacks will happen, but don't let them stop you. If you fall down, get back up; look at what other ways you can reach your destination.

20. Have courage. Remember you always have choices. The vast majority of the time, the things we fear most rarely happen. You can face it with God's help, your effort and your family and friend's support.

21. Be inspired. Read something inspiring every day, it may be your Holy Book, Prophetic sayings, or other contemporary literature.

WHEN YOU'RE SICK AND TIRED OF HAVING TRIED EVERYTHING

There are times when you may feel you gave it everything you had and you're still, as they say, "in the pits". Just as laziness is a problem, sometimes being over-zealous can be also. Backing off to take a break and regrouping is not a bad idea. Perseverance, although an important principle, needs to be balanced with flexibility. Sometimes you may be doing all the right things, but the light is still not shining at the end of the tunnel. Maybe there is light but instead of the break you were looking for, it feels like there is a locomotive heading your way. First of all, we are speaking metaphorically here. Make sure it is really not a locomotive and if it is…get out of the way!

Seriously though, there are no easy or quick-fix answers to the areas that have been covered. There are tried and tested principles but it takes determination, hope, timing and many other factors to ride the roller coaster through. However, in reality, not every problem has a clear solution.

At times like this, it becomes even more urgent to ask for help from family, friends, community or other professional organizations. Explore other options; no one said it is an easy ride. Remember, some people may let you down, others will be your backbone but most of all there's One support available toll-free, 24 hours a day—do not forget about Him! Keep asking for God's help. There are so many examples of Prophets and people gone by. Their stories should be an inspiration for us all, reminding us that we are not alone.

If You Persist

A Poem by JAVED MOHAMMED

Getting up is hard
I'm sure you'll agree
But if you persist
Then no one can keep you down

> Hit the Snooze button
> Stand up and salute another day
> Thank God for another chance another day

Doing the daily grind is hard
I'm sure you'll agree
But if you persist
Then each step will help you succeed

> Make the bed, make the effort
> Overcome your fears, overcome your laziness
> Here's another chance to do righteousness

Failing is hard
I'm sure you'll agree
But if you persist
Only then will you succeed

> Stand firm, stand upright
> Another rejection, Another refusal
> It's another chance to succeed

Looking for a way out is hard
I'm sure you'll agree
But if you persist
Then no difficulty will you see

Look near, look far
Another turn, another diversion
It's another chance for a new vision

Losing hope is hard
I'm sure you'll agree
But if you persist
Then God will make you trouble-free

Now the day is done
See what you did
If you persist, no snooze button can keep you down

Conclusion

NO EASY SHORT CUTS

Within the folds of history, there are many stories carrying examples from the past generations who practiced prayer and patience remarkably...

It is said that Khosrow, the Persian king, once was angry with one of his subjects, Bozorgmehr. Therefore, he detained him in a gloomy house and ordered to enchain him with iron. Several days later, the king sent some people to investigate his state. As they visited him in that gloomy house, they found him tranquil and cheerful. They were astonished and wondered, "How can you enjoy such peace of mind while you are in such a miserable state?" He answered, "In fact, I have made, mixed, and used six humors that helped me keep such manner. The first humor is trust in God. The second is to believe that every destined matter will inevitably occur. The third is the fact that steadfastness is the best thing the inflicted person should opt for. The fourth is the fact that what should I do if I do not practice patience, since I will not let impatience overtake me. The fifth is that there may be some others who suffer harsher calamities. The sixth is that relief may come in any moment."

Two of the six humors that Bozorgmehr made use of were patience and prayer. So what is prayer? What are its types? Are they really answered? Ask those who believe in it and you will hear the phrase "the power of prayer."

These are wise principles we can apply in life. We can see that in life, hardship and suffering should never come as a complete surprise. In fact, hardship is a certainty somewhere during our lifetime. It is a test of our faith and we should never despair. Self-pity leads us nowhere. Good fortune and misfortune are merely two sides of the same coin of life. Although we do not welcome hardship, we know that even in the afternoon of life, we live in the shadow of death. In the peak of our prosperity, we are just a few short paces away from poverty. In the prime of our good health; illness lurks in the shadows nearby. We should place our complete trust in God's abundance and have the certainty in heart and mind that at the end of our pain and suffering, God's love and mercy will embrace us.

Life is full of challenges, some of which may appear to be insurmountable. But with courage, determination, perseverance and prayers, the odds became insignificant.

I encourage you to be constantly asking yourselves: "What is the best use of my time? What is the best use of my wealth? What is the best use of the knowledge and talents God has blessed me with?"

Do not waste your time in endless discussions about problems you cannot influence. As an old Arab saying goes, "The action of one person which affects a thousand people is better than the talk of a thousand people which affects one person." So leverage your God-given gifts to benefit as many people as you can.

Do not let fear paralyze you from taking action. It is important to pause in life and reflect. But it is just as important to have faith, as faith beats fear. Move in the direction of your goals and persist at them until you reach them. And if you are in distress, ask for help.

Strength lies in unity, so let's start by focusing on first uniting our families and then our communities. Do not let petty things get magnified or let your egos get in the way of the greater good. Just as in the most intimate of relationships, there's give and take. We need to overlook each other's faults for those whose lives we touch. Be an optimist but also be practical.

Remember, the future belongs to those who are rich not in material things but in morals; not in technical wizardry but spiritual fulfillment; not those who take the most but those who give the most. We can all learn to let go and give the material to gain the spiritual.

The Caliph Ali once said, "You should always remember two things and you should always forget two things. You should always remember God and you should always remember death (an outcome we all have to face). And you should always forget the harm people have done towards you because it will build up rancor and ill feeling in your heart and you should always forget your good deeds so that you don't feel pride or arrogance." These are true words of wisdom.

Sometimes when we reflect on our situation, it may appear miserable. It reminds me of the analogy of a person who complains about his lot in life, all the problems and hardships. He is then given the opportunity to see the problems of other people. He looks at them one by one and then says, "Thank you, God; I am happy with my package!" This does not take away from addressing issues but it gives a sense of perspective and comfort that we can all think about.

In summary, having belief in God is a prerequisite. Being patient and offering prayers are the foundations. Having purpose leads to finding direction and meaning on your life. Planning your journey and taking action proactively give you the roadmap. Finally, passion is the fuel that propels you and gives you the perseverance to ride through the tough parts of this journey.

This book has presented principles, inspirational stories and practical ideas to make the principles into reality. In the end, these are tools that only have value if you use them. In order to use them effectively, you may have to re-read the book or certain chapters that really made sense to you. The principles and ideas have to be interpreted so they become meaningful goals and inspiration for you. The ideas have to go from "that's nice" to "hey, I can make a difference" by writing a plan, reviewing it often and building what works for your unique situation. In life, I am sure you are well aware that many times there are no easy short cuts.

May God give you and all of us the wisdom, stamina, health and well being to ride the roller coaster of life to our real success and well-being.

Appendix A

Inspiration from The Holy Qur'an

Sovereignty

"Say: O God! Owner of Sovereignty! Thou give sovereignty unto whom Thou wilt, and Thou withdraws sovereignty from whom Thou wilt. Thou exalts whom Thou wilt, and Thou abases whom Thou wilt. In Thy hand is the good. Lo! Thou art Able to do all things. Thou causes the night to pass into the day, and Thou causes the day to pass into the night. And Thou brings forth the living from the dead, and Thou brings forth the dead from the living. And Thou gives sustenance to whom Thou chooses, without stint." (3: 26-27)

Purpose

"Lo! In the creation of the heavens and the earth and (in) the difference of night and day are tokens (of His Sovereignty) for men of understanding, such as remember God, standing, sitting, and reclining, and consider the creation of the heavens and the earth, (and say): Our Lord! Thou creates not this in vain. Glory be to Thee! Preserve us from the doom of Fire." (3: 190-191)

Sustenance

"He who believes in Allah and the latter day; and whoever is careful of (his duty to) Allah, He will make for him an outlet. And give him sustenance from whence he thinks not; and whoever trusts in Allah, He is sufficient for him; surely Allah attains His purpose; Allah indeed has appointed a measure for everything." (65: 2-3)

"If God is your helper none can overcome you, and if He withdraw His help from you, who is there who can help you after Him? In God let believers put their trust." (3: 160)

"Race one with another for forgiveness from your Lord and a Garden whereof the breadth is as the breadth of the heavens and the earth, which is in store for those who believe in God and His messengers. Such is the bounty of God, which He bestows upon whom He will, and God is of Infinite Bounty." (57: 21)

"Have ye seen that which ye cultivate?
Is it ye who foster it, or are We the Fosterer?
If We willed, We verily could make it chaff,
then would ye cease not to exclaim
Lo! We are laden with debt! Nay, but we are deprived!
Have ye observed the water, which ye drink?
Is it ye who shed it from the rain cloud,
or are We the Shedder?
If We willed We verily could make it bitter.
Why then, give ye not thanks?
Have ye observed the fire which ye strike out?
Was it ye who made the tree thereof to grow,
or were We the grower?
We, even We, appointed it a memorial and a comfort for the dwellers in the wilderness." (56: 63-73)

"And verily thy Lord will give unto thee
so that thou wilt be content
Did He not find thee an orphan and protect (thee)?
Did He not find thee wandering and direct (thee)?
Did He not find thee destitute and enrich (thee)?
Therefore the orphan oppress not,
Therefore the beggar drive not away,
Therefore of the bounty of thy Lord be thy discourse."
(93 : 5-11)

"Trust in God's Mercy
The devil promises you destitution and enjoineth on you lewdness. But God promises you forgiveness from Himself with bounty. God is All-Embracing, All-knowing." (2: 268)

TESTS AND DIFFICULTIES

"Do men think that they will be left alone saying, We believe, and not be tried?" (29: 2)

"Do you think that you shall enter the Garden (of bliss) without such (trials) as came to those who passed away before you? They encountered suffering and adversity, and were so shaken in spirit that even the Messenger and those of faith who were with him cried: "When (will come) the help of God?" Ah! Verily, the help of God is (always) near!" (2: 214)

"God tasks not a soul beyond its scope. For it (is only) that which it hath earned, and against it (only) that which it hath deserved. Our Lord! Condemn us not if we forget, or miss the mark! Our Lord! Lay not on us such a burden as thou didst lay on those before us! Our Lord! Impose not on us that which we have not the strength to bear! Pardon us, absolve us and have mercy on us, Thou, our Protector, and give us victory over the disbelieving folk." (2: 286)

"And if we cause man to taste some mercy from Us and afterward withdraw it from him, lo! he is despairing, thankless. And if We cause him to taste grace after some misfortune that had befallen him, he says: The ills have gone from me. Lo! he is exultant, boastful; Save those who persevere and do good works. Theirs will be forgiveness and a great reward." (11: 9-11)

"Do men imagine that they will be left (at ease) because they say, We believe, and will not be tested with affliction? Lo! We tested those who were before you. Thus God knows those who are sincere, and knows those who feign. Or do those who do ill deeds imagine that they can outstrip Us? Evil (for them) is that which they decide. Whoso looks forward to the meeting with God (let him know that) God's reckoning is surely nigh, and He is the Hearer, the Knower." (29: 2-5)

"Man tires not of praying for good, and if ill touches him, then he is disheartened, desperate. And verily, if We cause him to taste mercy after some hurt that hath touched him, he will say: This is my own; and I deem not that the Hour will ever rise, and if I am brought back to my Lord, I surely shall be better off with Him - But We verily shall tell those who disbelieve (all) that they did, and We verily shall make them taste hard punishment." (41: 49-50)

"When We show favor unto man, he withdraws and turns aside, but when ill touches him then he abounds in prayer." (41: 51)

HARDSHIP AND EASE

"Verily, with every difficulty there is relief. Verily, with every difficulty there is relief." (94:5-6)

PATIENCE

"O ye who believe! Seek help in steadfastness and prayer. Lo! God is with the steadfast." (2.153)

GOOD WORDS

"A goodly saying, as a goodly tree, its root set firm, its branches reaching into heaven, Giving its fruit at every season by permission of its Lord? God coins the similitudes for mankind in order that they may reflect. And the similitude of a bad saying is as a bad tree, uprooted from upon the earth, possessing no stability." (14:25-26)

PERSONAL CONDUCT

"It is not righteousness that you turn your faces towards East or West.
But it is righteousness to believe in God and the Last Day,
And the Angels, and the Book, and the Messengers;
To spend of your substance, out of love for Him,
For your kin, for orphans, for the needy,
For the wayfarer, for those who ask,
and for the ransom of slaves;

To be steadfast in prayer
And give in charity;
To fulfill the contracts which you have made;
And to be firm and patient, in pain and adversity
And throughout all periods of panic.
Such are the people of truth, the God-fearing." (2: 177)

PATIENCE

"And verily, We shall bestow upon those who are patient the best rewards on account of what they did. And seek help through patience and surely this is a hard thing except for the humble ones." (2: 153)

"And surely we shall try you with something of fear and hunger and loss of wealth and lives and crops; but give glad tidings to those who patiently persevere." (2: 155)

"Most surely humankind is in loss except those who believe and do good works and enjoin upon one another Truth and patience." (103: 3)

"Only those who are patient shall receive their rewards in full without reckoning." (39: 10).

DEPENDENCE

"God is our support and the most excellent Patron." (2: 173)

"Whoever submits himself entirely to God and is the doer of good, he has his reward from his Lord." (2: 112)

"There is nothing for man but what he strives for." (65: 3)

"And it may be that you dislike a thing, which is good for you and that you like a thing, which is bad for you. God knows but you do not know." (2: 216)

"He provides for him from (sources) he never could imagine. And if any one puts his trust in God, sufficient is (God) for him." (65: 3)

"Say, nothing shall happen to us but what God has decreed for He is our Patron and in Him shall the faithful trust." (9: 51)

"And be steadfast in patience, for verily God will not suffer the reward of the righteous to perish." (11: 115)

"Be patient, for your patience is with the help of God. Nor grieve over them, and distress yourself not because of their plots. For God is with those who restrain themselves, and those who do good." (16: 127-128)

HATRED AND JUSTICE

"Oh you who believe!
Stand out firmly for God,
as witnesses to fair dealing.
And let not the hatred of others towards you
make you swerve to wrong and depart from justice.
Be just; that is next to piety." (5: 8)

PROPHETIC INSPIRATION

"Worship the Creator (without associating any partner with Him), be content with your provision and decrease the level of your expectations for this life."

"Wonderful is the affair of the believer. His affairs in their entirety are good for him. If good befalls him, he is thankful and that is good for him. And if harm befalls him, he is patient and that is good for him. And this (prosperous state of being) is only for the believer."

"If you ask, then ask God and if you seek help, then seek it from God. And know that if the whole of the nation were to rally together in order to bring benefit to you in anything, they would not benefit you except with that which God has written for you. And if they were to gather together in order to inflict harm upon you with something, they would not harm you except with that which God has written for you. The pen has been raised and the pages are dried."

"And know that what has befallen you was not going to miss you, and that which missed you was not meant to befall you."

"And know that victory comes with patience and that relief comes with hardship."

"Whoever spends the night safely in his place of sleep, is physically healthy and who has sufficient sustenance for his day, it is as if he achieved the world in its entirety."

"Be content with what God has apportioned for you and you will be the richest of people."

"Whoever's main concern becomes the Hereafter, God will make things well for him and will make richness to dwell in his heart. And the world will come to him despite its unwillingness. Whoever's main concern becomes this world, God will scatter his affairs and will place poverty between his eyes and the world will not come to him, except what was written for him."

"Love and remember God in good times, He will remember you in hard times."

"If you had all relied upon God with implicit trust, he would certainly have given you your livelihood as He supplied provision to the birds that awake hungry in the morning and return with full bellies at dusk."

"Surely God is the Great Giver of sustenance, possessing absolute power, the All Mighty."

"From the rights of mutual love is to forgive and overlook shortcomings."

"Do not be people without minds of your own, saying that if others treat you well you will treat them well, and that if they do wrong you will do wrong. Rather, accustom yourselves to do good if people do good and not to do wrong if they do evil."

"No one should wish for death because of any misfortune that befalls him. If anybody should be so much hard up with life he should say: 'O God! Keep me alive so long as life is good for me and take my life so long as death is better for me.' "

"The strong one is not he who overcomes his adversary. Verily, the strong one is he who overcomes his anger."

"God, the Glorious, says: 'I have no better reward than Paradise for a believing servant of mine who is patient and resigned when I take away one of his beloved ones.' "

"For any trouble, illness, worry, grief, hurt or sorrow which afflicts a Muslim—even the pricking of a thorn—God removes in its stead some of his sins."

"When God wishes good to His servant, He hastens punishment for him in this world and when God wishes evil, He lets him off in this world for his sin until the Day of Judgment."

"Nine things the Lord has commanded me: Fear of God in private and in public; Justness, whether in anger or in calmness; Moderation in both poverty and affluence; Joining hands with those who break away from me; Giving to those who deprive me; Forgiving those wrong me; Making of my silence meditation; Making my words remembrance of God; And taking a lesson from my observation."

THE PROPHET'S PRAYER

"O God, I complain to you of my weakness, lack of resources and humiliation before men. You are the most merciful, You are the Lord of the oppressed and You are my Lord. To whom will you entrust me? To someone far away who will frown on me or to an enemy to whom you have given power over me? If you are not angry with me, I do not care, but Your favor is better for me. I seek refuge with the light of Your face, which illuminates the darkness, and by which the affairs of this world and the next are put in order, from having Your anger descend on me or Your wrath fall upon me. I repent to You, seeking Your forgiveness and Your favor until You are well pleased. There is neither power nor strength except by God."

"O God! I seek refuge in Thee from anxiety, grief, incapacity, laziness, stinginess, cowardice, from the burden of debt and from the domination of people."

Appendix B

Memorable Quotes

Four things come not back: the spoken word, the spent arrow, the past, the neglected opportunity. — *Omar Idn Al-Halif*

It's fine to celebrate success, but it is more important to heed the lessons of failure. — *Bill Gates*

The last dejected effort often becomes the winning stroke. — *Unknown*

Some men give up their designs when they have almost reached the goal while others, on the contrary, obtain a victory by exerting, at the last moment, more vigorous efforts than ever before. — *Herodotus*

Many of life's failures are people who did not realize how close they were to success when they gave up. — *Thomas Edison*

You may be disappointed if you fail, but you are doomed if you don't try. — *Beverly Sills*

Not everything that is faced can be changed, but nothing can be changed until it is faced. — *James Baldwin*

He who endures conquers. — *Italian Proverb*

If you want to succeed in life...you must pick 3 bones to carry with you at all times a wishbone, a backbone, and a funny bone. – *Reba McEntire*

What lies behind us and lies before us are small matters compared to what lies within us. – *Ralph Waldo Emerson*

A positive attitude is like a fire: unless you continue to add fuel, it goes out. – *Alexander Lockhart*

We learn to walk by stumbling. – *Bulgarian Proverb*

People in distress will sometimes prefer a problem that is familiar to a solution that is not. – *Neil Postman*

The past should be a springboard not a hammock.
– *Irving Ball*

When I hear somebody sigh that "Life is hard," I am always tempted to ask, "Compared to what?" – *Sydney Harris*

Do not look back in anger, or forward in fear, but around in awareness. – *Unknown*

Don't undermine your worth by comparing yourself with others. – *Unknown*

Reflect upon your present blessings, of which every man has many, not on your past misfortune, of which all men have some. – *Charles Dickens*

Think like a man of action, act like a man of thought.
– *Henri Bergson*

You cannot shake hands with a clenched fist. – *Indira Gandhi*

A good teacher, like a good entertainer, first must hold his audience's attention. Then he can teach the lesson.
– *John Henrik Clarke*

It is truly said: It does not take much strength to do things, but it requires great strength to decide what to do.
– *Chow Ching*

Be like a postage stamp: stick to one thing until you get there!
– *Unknown*

Appendix C

Appendix

REFERENCES

The material for this book was researched from many sources. The following are the major references.

Shiraz and The Dove adapted from www.thenlightenment.com

Prophet Job from www.angelfire.com/on/ummiby1/job.html

Awqaaf by Hamza Yusuf from a 1999 ING speech

The Illustrated Rumi by Philip Dunn et-all

Unstoppable by Cynthia Kersey

The Greatest Sales Training in the World by Robert Nelson, et al

Don't be Sad by Shaykh Aaidh ibn Abdullah Al-Qarni

Few Women 'Happy With Their Bodies' from news.bbc.co.uk

How Beautiful is Beautiful by Luke Tagg, www.tashitagg.co.za

When Does Gold Become Ore:
    Traveling the Path of Love by Bhai Sahib

Simply Beautiful: Choosing an Uncluttered, Focused, Rich Life
    by Sam Quick, Kentucky Cooperative Extension

The Psychology of Happiness from www.globalideasbank.org

How to Be Happy from www.evolutionary-economics.org

The Road to Resilience from the American Psychological Association,
helping.apa.org

Suddenly Unemployed by Helen K. hosier

Enduring Hardship sermon
by Arshad Gamiet at the Royal Holloway College

Don't Sweat the Small Stuff by Richard Carlson

Relax, You May Only Have a Few Minutes Left by Loretta Laroche